BACKGAMMON
THE
CRUELEST GAME

W9-AMU-431

Barclay Cooke & Jon Bradshaw

BACKGAMMON THE CRUELEST GAME

RANDOM HOUSE

New York

To Madora

Endpaper illustrations courtesy of Culver Pictures

Copyright © 1974 by Barclay Cooke and Jon Bradshaw

All rights reserved under International and Pan-American Copyright Conventions.
Published in the United States by Random House, Inc., New York, and simultaneously
in Canada by Random House of Canada Limited, Toronto.

Cooke, Barclay.
Backgammon: The Cruelest Game.
1. Backgammon. I. Bradshaw, Jon, joint author.
II. Title.
GV1469.B2C66   795′.1   74-8725
ISBN 0-394-48812-1
ISBN 0-394-73243-X pbk.
Manufactured in the United States of America

Design by Bernard Klein

6897

CONTENTS

BACKGAMMON
THE
CRUELEST GAME

◄1►
THE RULES OF THE GAME

Everything is very simple in war, but the
simplest thing is difficult.
—*Karl von Clausewitz*

Though backgammon is one of the most deceptive and difficult of board games and *the* most cunning game of chance, its rules are few and simple and its objectives are easily understood.

The game is normally played by two opponents (though more than two may play in what is known as *chouette*) on a board divided into four sections or quadrants. Each quadrant is marked with six alternately colored triangles called *points*. (See Diagram 1.) Each point has its designated number ranging from 1 to 12 on either side of the board, totaling 24 points in all. These points are referred to by their numbers, as, for example, the 1 point or the 6 point. Only the 7 point actually has a name and is called the *bar point*, since it is next to the bar that divides the board in two. The colors of the points have no significance other than to distinguish one from the other.

Each opponent has fifteen men, or checkers; for the purposes of this book, one opponent's men will be red, the other white. It might be simpler and would certainly be accurate to imagine these men as two opposing armies.

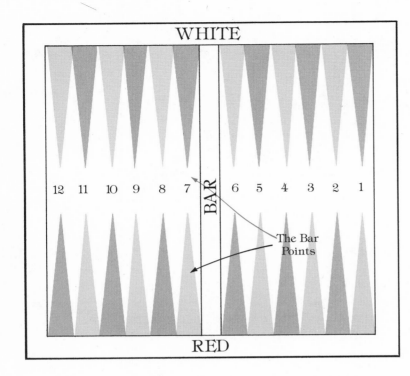

WHITE

12 11 10 9 8 7 BAR 6 5 4 3 2 1

The Bar
Points

RED

Diagram
1

When the game begins, the two armies are arranged on either side of the board in battle-line formations. (See Diagram 2.) As is apparent, one side is the mirror image of the other. Since, theoretically, it does not matter in which direction you move your men, the board might be set up in exactly the opposite way. (See Diagram 3.) There is no difference between the opening arrangements, but custom dictates that both of the players' inner boards be nearer the source of light. It is an old custom, almost certainly derived from the fact that backgammon, like many other gambling games, tended to be nocturnal and was often played in ill-lit rooms.

Dependent on the rolls of the dice, the object of the game is, as illustrated in Diagram 2, for white to move his men forward in a clockwise direction around and off the

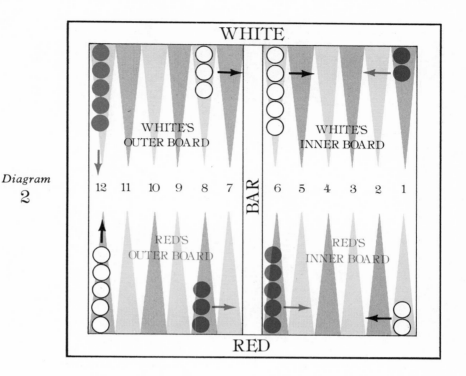

Diagram
2

board before red, moving in a counterclockwise direction, can do the same. The men are not permitted to move backwards. Before either player may take any men off, all fifteen of his men must be in his inner board. Taking men off the board is called *bearing off*.

If white, for example, can accomplish this (that is, move his army around and off the board) before red, white wins the game. If white can do this before red has moved all of his men into his own inner board, and has borne at least one man off, white wins a double game or what is called a *gammon*. And, should white accomplish this with any of red's men remaining in white's inner board, white will win a triple game or a *backgammon*. The triple game, incidentally, is an American amendment and is not recognized in England or on the Continent.

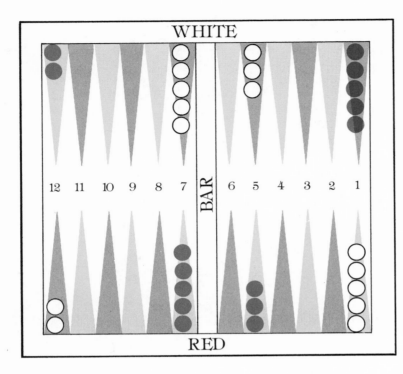

Diagram
3

The men are moved in strict accordance with the rolls of the dice. At the start of every game, each player rolls one die, and the player who has rolled the higher number has the opportunity of playing first—using both resulting numbers. Each player must roll his die into the board at his right. If the dice do not come to rest flat on the board—that is, if either die is angled up against the side of the board or against one of the checkers—it is called *cocked* and must be rolled again. If both players roll the same number, they must re-roll until different numbers appear. Following the opening roll, the players take alternate turns, and each rolls both his dice together.

Let us assume that player A has rolled a 6 and player B a 2. Because player A has rolled the higher number, he is entitled to play first. He has two separate ways in which

to play the 6 and 2; he can move one of his men forward 6
points and another up 2 points, or, using the sum total of
the dice, he can move one man 8 points. Either number
may be played first. In other words, a roll of 6 and 2 may be
played in either of two ways — as a 6-2 or as a 2-6. If, however, a situation arises where only one number can be
moved and there is a choice, it is mandatory to play the
higher one. Let's assume white rolls a 6-2 and that if he
plays the 6, he has no way to move the 2 and vice versa. He
must play the 6 in this instance and forgo the 2. If either
player rolls a double — for example, double 4's — he is
obliged to move that number four times if possible. That
is, he can move one man 16 points or two men 8 points or
two men 4 points and another two men 4 points. This
principle applies to all doubles. In their simplest variations,
these are the basic mechanics employed in the movement of
all the pieces.

The men are permitted to land on any point which is
not already occupied by two or more of the other player's
men. Such *blocks*, as they are called, by two or more of the
other player's men, make or establish the point; they resemble fortified positions, which, so long as there are at
least two enemy men on any one point, remain impregnable. Thus, if player A rolled a 6 and player B had formed a
block 6 points away, player A would not be permitted to
land on that position. If, however, he rolled a 6 and a 3, for
example, he could, provided there were no other enemy
blocks further along, leap across the block by using the 3
first and then the 6. This point is illustrated in Diagram 4.
Here, white has rolled a 6-3 and wishes to move one of
his men on the 1 point forward. Had he rolled two 6's, he
would not have been able to get beyond red's fortified position. But, by employing the 3 first, he is able to hurdle it.

Blocks are crucial to the playing of backgammon. The
more consecutive blocks a player can build, the greater

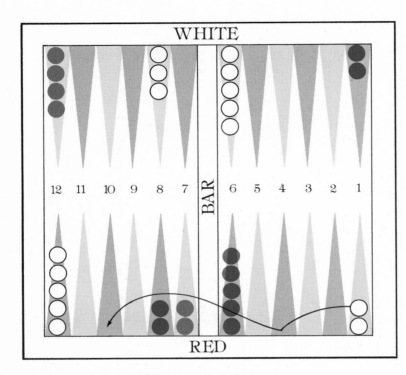

Diagram
4

chance he has of imprisoning any of his opponent's men behind them. They are the military equivalent of a series of tightly formed barricades. A six-point block—that is, two men positioned on each of six consecutive points—constitutes what is called a *prime*. Because the largest number a player can roll is a 6, a prime prevents the enemy from hurdling over it. An example of a prime is shown in Diagram 5. Obviously, any lesser number of consecutive blocks, such as a four- or a five-point block, is not as strong as a prime, but is very valuable in restricting the movement of enemy men.

Men which are not a part of a block—that is, those men occupying points by themselves—are called *blots*. In military terms, such men resemble stragglers, who are either lost or have become separated from the main body of

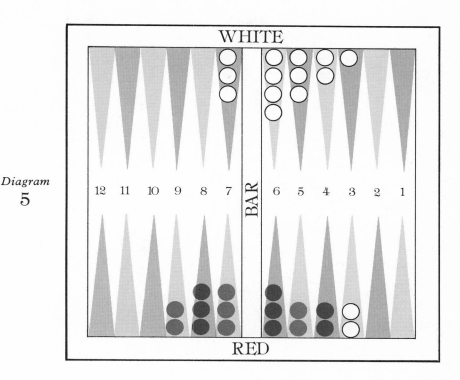

Diagram 5

their army, and as a result are relatively easy targets of attack. In Diagram 6, for example, the enemy, providing he rolls the exact number (in this instance, a 3-6 or 4-5), can land on red's open man, or blot. This form of capture is called *hitting a blot*. Any open and unprotected man is a potential prisoner. (Often, however, it is not as foolhardy as it may appear to leave blots intentionally in order to increase your options of movement, but this is a more subtle tactical maneuver, which we will discuss in subsequent chapters.)

Since a player must complete his full roll—that is, play both numbers—and since it is not always possible to land safely on your own secure positions, both are often forced to leave blots up and down the board. If one of your blots is captured by your opponent, regardless of how far

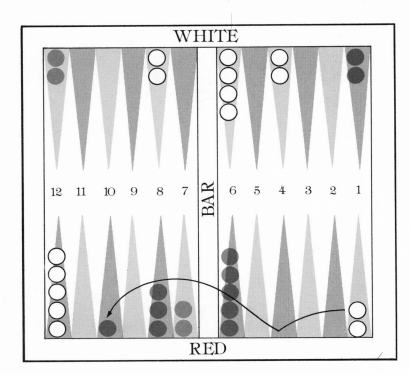

WHITE

| 12 | 11 | 10 | 9 | 8 | 7 | BAR | 6 | 5 | 4 | 3 | 2 | 1 |

RED

Diagram
6

your man has advanced, he is sent back to the beginning (or, as it is called, *put on the bar*). The captured man is literally placed upon the bar that divides the board and must remain there until he is able to enter the game again. Given the continual struggle being waged up and down the board, it is possible for both players to have captured men on the bar at the same time, and for one player, or both, to have several men on the bar.

Captured men are permitted to re-enter the game only when they have rolled a number that corresponds to the number of a point in their opponent's inner board which is not occupied by two or more of the opponent's men. For example, in Diagram 7, one of white's men has been captured and has been placed on the bar. Since red has established blocks on his 6 and 5 points, white, should he

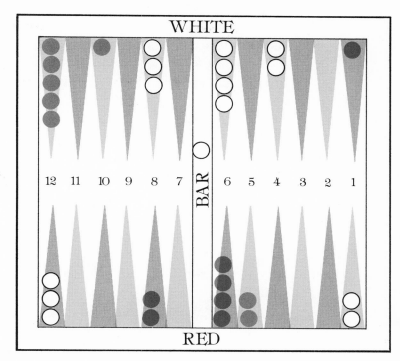

Diagram 7

roll either a 6 or a 5, would not be able to come in on either of those two points. Specifically, if he rolled a 6-5, double 5's or double 6's, he could not come in at all. A roll of 6-2, however, would mean that he could come in on the 2 point, but not on the 6 point, and would have to play his 6 elsewhere. Obviously, then, the more blocks a player can erect in his inner board (assuming that at least one of the enemy men has been captured), the less chance his opponent will have of re-entering the game.

In the ideal defensive position, red blocks all the points in his inner board, establishing what is called a *closed board.* Should white have a captured man on the bar, he will not be able to re-enter the game at all—at least until red decides or is forced into opening one of his points. This is one of the game's main strategies—to capture one or more of your opponent's men and to close your board completely, thereby shutting off all means of escape. For as long as either player has a man on the bar, he is not permitted to move elsewhere until that man is returned to play. A closed board, then, is the perfect defensive position, equivalent to a naval blockade.

The final method of moving your men is when you actually bear them off the board. When the game begins, it is already one-third over in one sense, since five of your fifteen men are already in your inner board. The object of the game, as previously explained, is to move all the rest of your men around and into your inner board. Only when all are in can you begin bearing them off, and the player who gets all of them off first wins the game.

Again, the men are borne off in accordance with the numbers shown on the rolled dice. As in the three other sections, there are six points in your inner board. Assume that you have moved all of your men into your inner board as shown in Diagram 8. If white now rolls a 4-2, he is permitted to take one man off his 4 point and another off his 2 point. If he rolls double 4's, he is permitted to take three men off his 4 point and can then move his remaining 4 down four points from the 6 point or down four points from his 5 point. Because there was not a fourth 4 on his 4 point, he is not able to bear another man off. This would also hold true had he rolled a 1. As there are no men on his 1 point, he will have to move a 1 elsewhere in his inner board. You must use your entire roll. For example, if white did not have any men on his 6 point and rolled a 6, he would take one man off his next lowest point on which there were men. This rule is implemented on a descending scale, so that if, for example, white has only two men left on his 1 point and he rolls a 6-5, he can take them both off. The same rule applies to doubles. To repeat: the

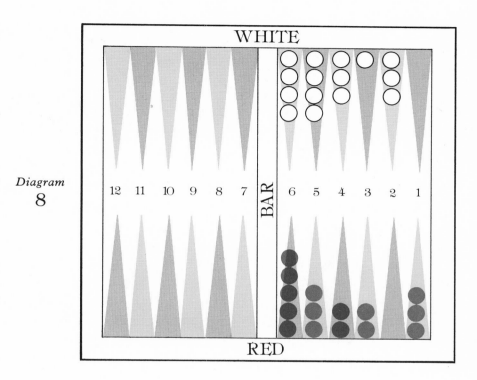

Diagram
8

WHITE

12 11 10 9 8 7 BAR 6 5 4 3 2 1

RED

player who bears off all of his men first wins the game.

These, then, are the simple, almost nursery-game rules of backgammon. Of course the game's apparent simplicity is its initial attraction. But its simplicity is of infinite variety, and is an amalgam of science and art. As with any dice game, luck plays its customary role. Skill is employed first by learning the rules and then by knowing the percentages and probabilities—when to play offense or defense, when to block and when to run. But it is important to understand these fundamentals before going on to more arcane and complicated matters. There is much more to backgammon than what the Penguin *Dictionary of English* innocently defines as "a hinged board with draughtsmen and dice," but it is well to begin with that.

◄2►

BASIC OPENING MOVES AND A FEW ESSENTIAL REPLIES

*Whatever is to the advantage of one side
is to the disadvantage of the other.*
— Karl von Clausewitz

As explained in the previous chapter, once each player has cast his opening die, the player who has rolled the higher number begins the game, using both his and his opponent's numbers. Thus, if player A has rolled a 2 and player B a 6, player B must now play a 6 and a 2. These are the game's opening shots, the initial sally into the battlefield, and they should not be played at random.

As in any conflict, at the outset there are certain sound strategic moves to be made, and since these moves will almost certainly influence the enemy's subsequent actions, they must be utilized to your best advantage. Immediately, therefore, a campaign strategy must be devised, the sole purpose of which is the ultimate surrender or destruction of the enemy forces.

The opening moves are the first step in this direction and, unlike other parts of the game, they should almost always be played in certain tactical ways. These moves can and should be learned by rote. They are simple but important ploys, the aim of which is to seek or establish strong opening positions.

Depending on the dice, of course, there are both favorable and unfavorable opening rolls, and the odds, alas, are 25 to 11 (coincidentally, the most familiar fraction in backgammon, which you will get to know well in Chapter Four) against obtaining a favorable opening roll. The good opening rolls are any double (except double 5's), 3-1, 4-2 and 6-1. (Theoretically, only the second player can open with a double.) These rolls establish strong positions or beachheads from which it is possible to launch subsequent assaults. All other rolls, in varying degree, are unfavorable. In our view, 6-5 is an unfavorable opening roll, since it leaves the back man unprotected and contributes nothing to the strengthening of your position. In fact, *any* 5 on the opening roll is weak and inauspicious.

In order of preference the opening rolls are

1-1	6-2
6-6	6-4
3-3, 4-4, 2-2	6-3
3-1	5-5
4-2, 6-1	2-1, 4-1
6-5	5-1
3-2	5-4
4-3	5-2
5-3	

To repeat: the opening moves should almost always be played in the same way. We say "almost," since, if you are rolling second, you may have to alter certain moves in order to combat the opening roll of your opponent. (These tactics will be discussed later in the chapter.)

Assuming you are playing first, the opening rolls should be played in the manner suggested below. (Go back and consult the opening position shown in Diagram 2 and assume that you are red.)

1-1 — Bring two men from red's 8 point to red's 7, or bar point, and two men from red's 6 point to red's 5 point. This invaluable roll establishes an immediate three-point block incorporating two important points — red's bar point and 5 point. There is no better way of playing this best of all opening rolls. (See Diagram 9.)

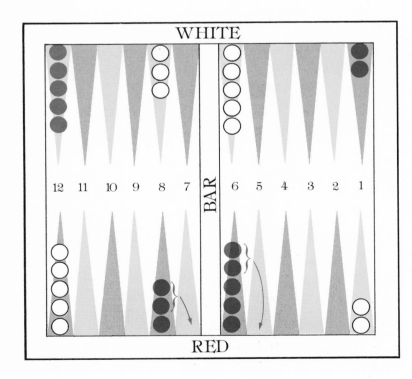

Diagram
9

WHITE

12 11 10 9 8 7 BAR 6 5 4 3 2 1

RED

6-6 — Bring two men from white's 1 point to white's bar point and two men from white's 12 point to red's bar point. You have now established superb offensive and defensive positions and are off to a commanding lead. (See Diagram 10.)

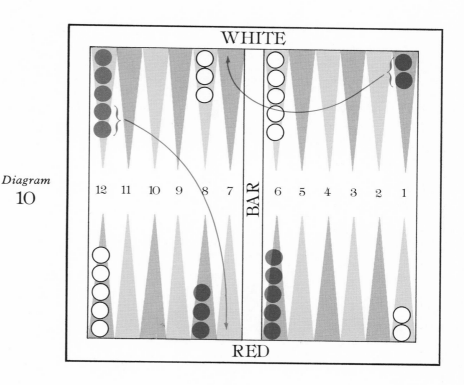

Diagram
10

3-3 — Bring two men from red's 8 point to red's 5 point and two men from white's 1 point to white's 4 point. With this roll there are alternative plays. Some favor moving two men from white's 12 point to red's bar point, but this play may best be described as atrocious. Though it does block sixes rolled by your opponent, your own bar point is not that important this early in the game. More importantly, there are better plays. Another alternative is to bring two men from red's 8 point to red's 5 point and two men from red's 6 point down to red's 3 point—thereby giving red three immediate points in his inner board. It is a good offensive play, but second-best. Our recommended play achieves two immediate advantages: a good offense and a good defense. Its alternative

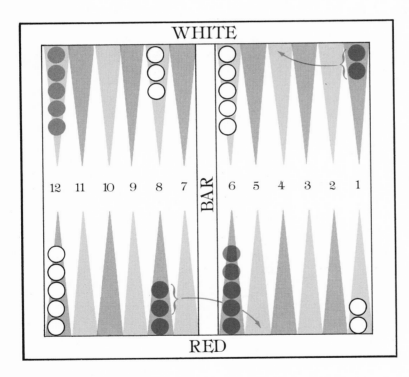

Diagram **11**

(making the two points in red's inner board) might be effectively employed in a tournament, for example, should red require a double game,* but in most

*This will be discussed in Chapter Seven.

cases your position is not considerably improved by making the extra point, particularly in view of the other, better defensive play of bringing two men up from white's 1 point. An additional advantage of this play is that it renders white's 5 point, should he make it early in the game, much less valuable than it would normally be. (See Diagram 11.)

4-4 — Bring two men from white's 1 point up to white's 5 point and two men from red's 8 point down to red's 4 point. It is true that the blot on red's 8 point now becomes vulnerable to any roll of white's totaling 7, but it also negates his ordinarily good roll of 6-1,

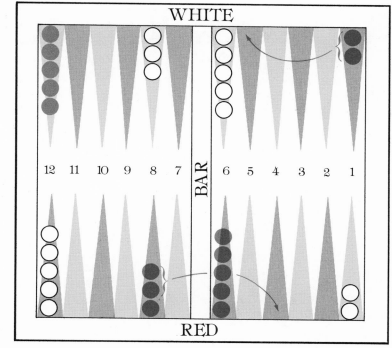

Diagram
12

since he will probably use it to hit red rather than making his own bar point. Our recommended play employs the best offensive and defensive tactics. Instead of the 4 point, most experts recommend making red's 9 point, but we prefer the former play. (See Diagram 12.)

2-2 — Our recommended play is to bring two men from white's 12 point to red's 11 point and two men from red's 6 point to red's 4 point. This is a strong attacking position. Alternatively, should you have less experience than your opponent, you might bring

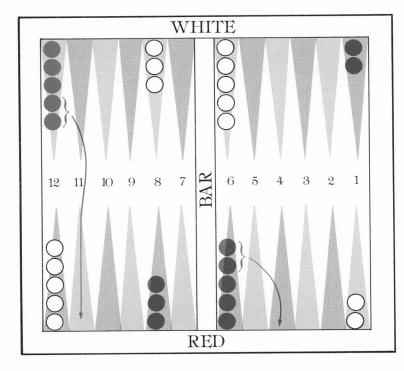

Diagram
13

two men up from white's 1 point to white's 5 point. It is seldom wrong to make your opponent's 5 point, and it is an excellent defensive position. Double 2's probably have more "correct" variations than any other double on the opening roll. (See Diagram 13.)

3-1 — This is the golden shot to make the golden point. Move one man from red's 8 point to red's 5 point and one man from red's 6 point to red's 5 point. Excluding doubles, there is no more advantageous opening roll. (See Diagram 14.)

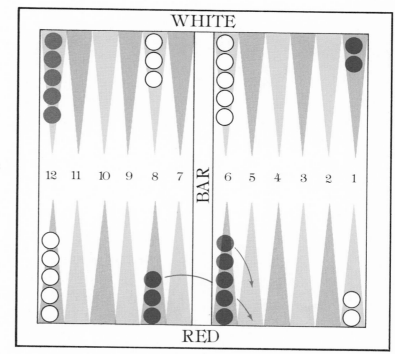

Diagram
14

4-2 — Bring one man from red's 8 point to red's 4 point
and another man from red's 6 point to red's 4 point,
thereby establishing red's 4 point. Since this roll
establishes a valuable point in red's inner board, it
is every bit as good a roll as 6-1, although probably
not considered so by many players. (See Diagram 15.)

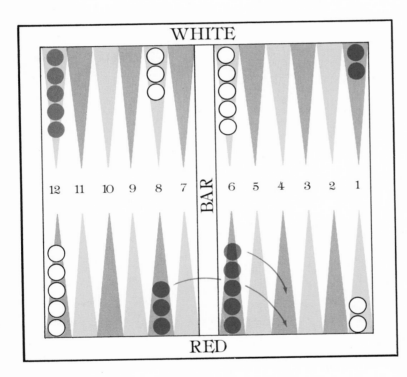

Diagram
15

6-1 — Bring one man from white's 12 point to red's bar
point and one man from red's 8 point to red's bar
point. This is a strong play, creating a three-point
block, but it accomplishes no immediate objective
other than to block sixes. However, there are no
real alternatives, though some experts when seeking

involvement against weaker players have been known to move one man from white's 12 point to their bar point and another man from their 6 point to their 5 point, thereby leaving two directly assaultable blots. It is a droll but insupportable play and is not to be recommended. (See Diagram 16.)

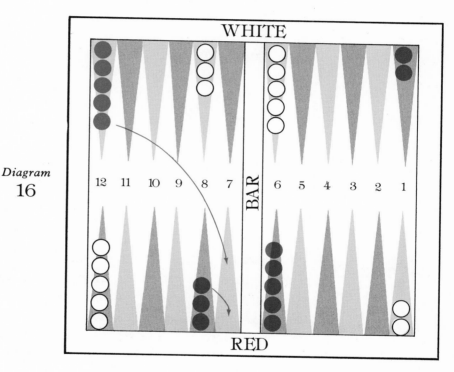

Diagram **16**

6-5 — Bring one man from white's 1 point all the way out to white's 12 point. In backgammon parlance, this move is referred to as the *lover's leap*. There is no good alternative. The 6-5 separates the favorable from the unfavorable rolls. It is not particularly advantageous and it forces red into an early running game. (See Diagram 17.)

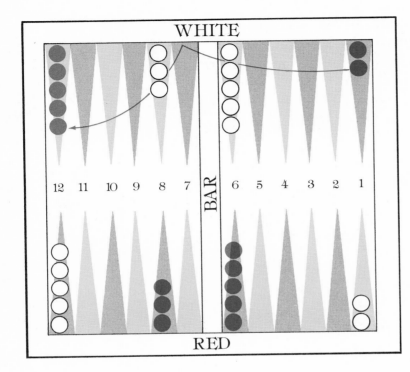

WHITE

| 12 | 11 | 10 | 9 | 8 | 7 | BAR | 6 | 5 | 4 | 3 | 2 | 1 |

Diagram
17

RED

3-2 — Bring two men down from white's 12 point, placing one of them on red's 11 point and the other on red's 10 point. Since red is vulnerable only to a roll of 9 or 10 by white, he is relatively secure and in an excellent position to create additional points. There is an alternative—bringing one man from white's 12 point to red's 11 point and dropping one man from red's 8 point to red's 5 point. If red is not hit, he is in a good position to make his 5 point on his next roll. But a roll of 4 will hit and double 4's could be a serious blow. The first play is superior. (See Diagram 18.)

Diagram **18**

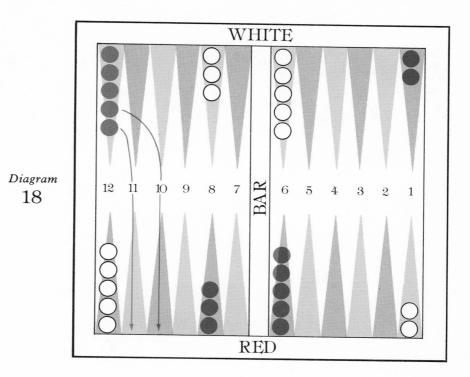

4-3 — Bring two men from white's 12 point to red's 9 and 10 points. Again, this gives red the potential to create new points. Although vulnerable to rolls totaling 8 or 9, this is still the most effective play. There are no happier alternatives. (See Diagram 19.)

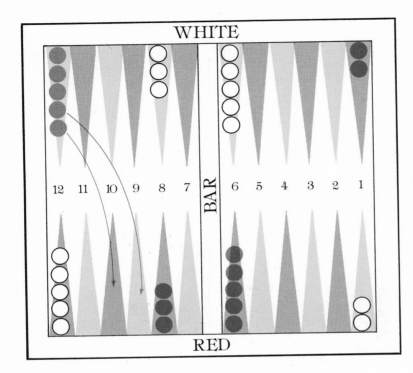

Diagram
19

5-3 — Bring down two men from white's 12 point, placing them on red's 8 and 10 points. It is true that your blot is vulnerable to a roll of 9, but should it not be hit, this play, on red's next move, changes lackluster rolls of 5-1, 4-1, 6-3, 6-2 or another 5-3 into good rolls. It also improves subsequent rolls of 4-3, 3-2 and 2-1. Some experts have suggested establishing red's 3 point with a roll of 5-3, but it is an inferior play. At this point in the game, the 3 point is almost irrelevant; it does not become really valuable until the 5 and 4 points have been secured. (See Diagram 20.)

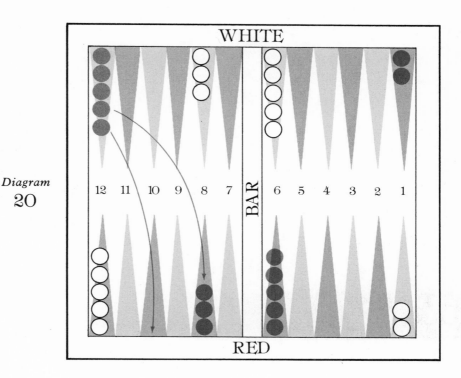

Diagram
20

6-2 — Bring one man from white's 12 point all the way to
red's 5 point. To bring one man from white's 1 point
out to white's 9 point is not as good a play. Both
plays can be hit by a 4, though double 1's cannot hit
the 6-2 brought out to white's 9 point. Although
double 1's can hit the exposed man on red's 5 point,
a good player would never make this play, so the odds
in both instances are even. At this early stage in the
game, it is well worth gambling to secure red's 5 point.
Red is exposed only to a roll of 4 or a combination
totaling 4. Any other alternatives are even less satisfactory. (See Diagram 21.)

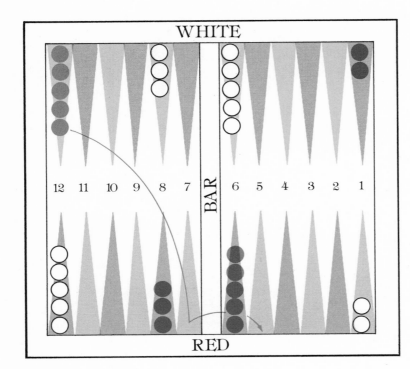

Diagram
21

6-4 — Bring one man from white's 1 point to white's 11 point. In this play red is exposed to a direct 2, but if not hit, he has released one man and placed him in a position to create new points in his outer board. It is not recommended that red make his 2 point with this roll. Such a play accomplishes nothing except to advance two men too far too early. (See Diagram 22.)

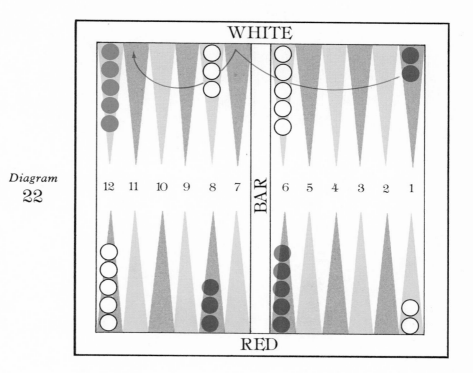

Diagram
22

6-3 — Bring one man from white's 1 point out to white's
10 point. There is no satisfactory alternative. Red is
now vulnerable to a direct 3. This is a shade worse
than 6-4, since it is 25 to 11 that a 2 will not be hit
but 23 to 13 that the exposed 3 will not be hit. Nonetheless, it is the best way to play this altogether un-
satisfactory roll. (See Diagram 23.)

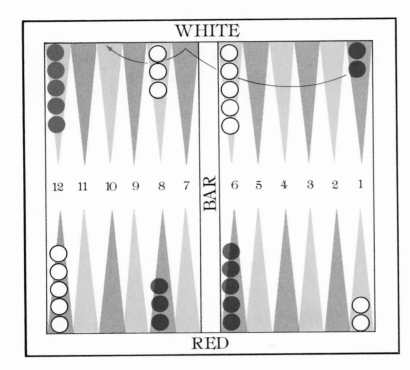

Diagram
23

5-5 — Bring two men from white's 12 point all the way to red's 3 point. This roll is the most odious of doubles. It accomplishes relatively little and forces two men more or less out of position. It becomes especially awkward when followed by further 5's. (See Diagram 24.)

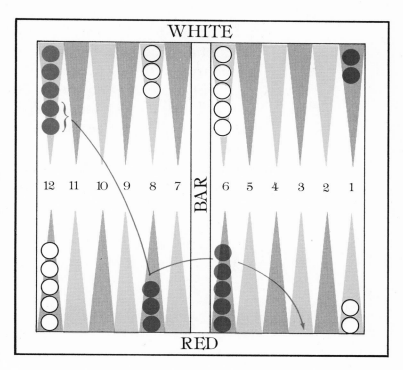

Diagram
24

2-1—Bring one man from white's 12 point to red's 11 point and another man from red's 6 point to red's 5 point. This is an unfortunate roll, but red has no better option than to attempt to secure his 5 point. He is exposed to a direct 4, but if he is not hit, his chances of establishing his 5 point are much improved. Under no circumstances should red split his back men by moving a man from white's 1 point to white's 2 point. At this stage in the game, white's 1 point is red's main security. Were red to separate those two men, he would become vulnerable to double 5's, and a 4-1. Dropping an exposed man on red's 5 point is considered bold by the inexperienced player. In fact, it is less bold than separating the two men on white's 1 point, for in addition to the threat of double 5's and a 4-1, red's back men are also exposed to the threat of double 4's and double 6's. Such rolls will occur only 5 out of 36 times, but why give white even that chance? In the beginning of the game, it could well be the end. In our recommended play, red is open to attack from any 4 and could lose both men should his opponent roll a 6-4—white's perfect shot. But even if red then rolled double 6's and was unable to re-enter, he would still be in the game because he commands that one defensive point in white's inner board. Our initial suggestion is the superior play. (See Diagram 25.)

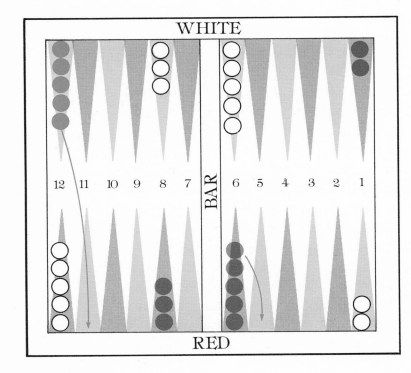

Diagram
25

WHITE

12 11 10 9 8 7 BAR 6 5 4 3 2 1

RED

4-1 — Bring one man from white's 12 point to red's 9 point and drop another man from red's 6 point to red's 5 point. This is a good offensive move. Again red is exposed to a 4, and double 4's would capture both men, but it is still the best play. The problem with both the 4-1 and the 2-1 is that nothing constructive is immediately accomplished. Red is only preparing to make points and is therefore vulnerable. Even so, should the blots not be hit, red's position is potentially strong. (See Diagram 26.)

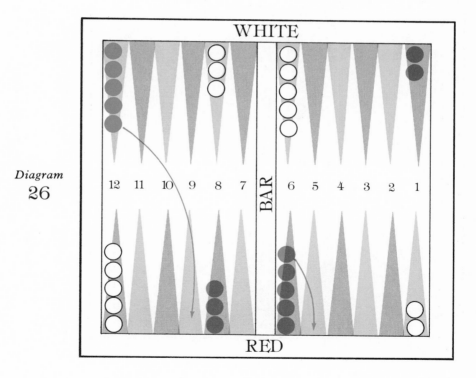

Diagram
26

WHITE

12 11 10 9 8 7 BAR 6 5 4 3 2 1

RED

5-1 — Bring one man from white's 12 point to red's 8 point and drop another man from red's 6 point to red's 5 point. All opening 5's are clumsy; any other roll has greater promise. An alternative play would be to bring a man from white's 12 point to red's bar point, but this is not as valuable a point to attempt to secure at this early stage of the game. Although unsafe, it is best to gamble in order to secure the important 5 point. Again, red should not split the two men on white's 1 point; the risks are serious and the rewards slight. (See Diagram 27.)

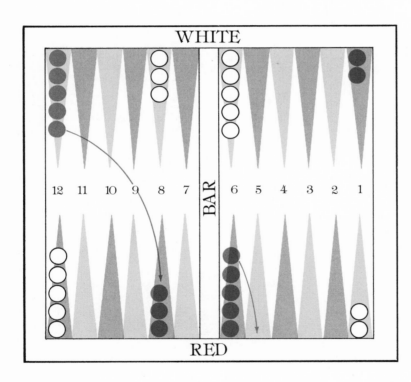

Diagram
27

5-4 — Bring two men from white's 12 point to red's 9 and 8 points. Red is exposed to any 8, but it is a better play than bringing one man from white's 1 point out to white's 10 point, where red would be vulnerable to a direct 3. Red has acquired nine *pips* (or points) and should not relinquish them lightly. The one drawback to our recommended play is that red adds an irrelevant man to his 8 point, but the play is preferred for the extra builder he acquires on his 9 point. (See Diagram 28.)

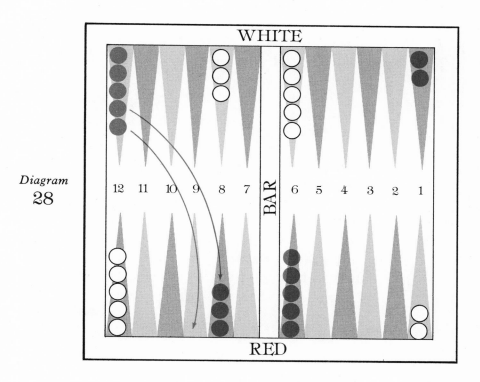

Diagram
28

WHITE

12 11 10 9 8 7 BAR 6 5 4 3 2 1

RED

5-2 — Bring two men from white's 12 point to red's 11 and 8 points. This is the worst of opening rolls. There are no good alternative plays. (See Diagram 29.)

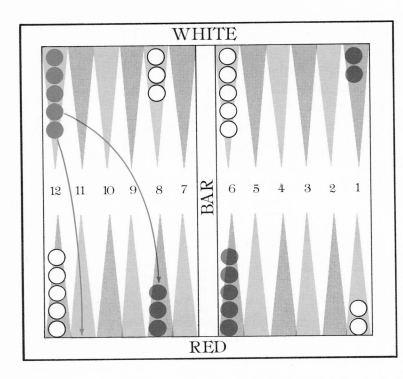

Diagram
29

At this stage, having recommended certain basic opening moves, we will explain just why we believe them to be correct—or at least why they are sounder than their alternatives. Backgammon is a game of infinite variations, of specific departures and deviations from general rules of thumb, and even the opening moves are affected by this phenomenon. For as long as backgammon has been played, there has been a difference of opinion as to the "correct" deployment of the various opening rolls. To this day, only 8 of the 21 opening rolls are generally agreed upon—1-1, 5-5, 6-6, 3-1, 4-2, 6-1, 6-5 and 5-2. The other 13 all seem to have acceptable alternatives and are played differently by different players. In each case where no certainty has existed, it has been our aim to give what we believe to be the best tactical alternative.

For instance, for years it was thought correct with opening rolls of 5-1, 4-1 and 2-1 to use the 1 to split the two men in the opponent's inner board; few players deployed the 1 in any other way. Gradually, however, the alternative of using the 1 to start your own 5 point was employed, and both moves began to seem equally advantageous. After continual study and analysis, we are now firmly convinced that a player should not split those back men immediately. The paradox of the "gambling" play of starting your 5 point, as opposed to the "conservative" play of splitting the back men, is intriguing, for in reality, the split is infinitely more of a gamble than its alternative.

But since we are so against the splitting of the back men, why do we recommend coming out all the way with opening rolls of 6-3 and 6-4? The remaining back man is vulnerable to double 5's, and it is quite possible that both blots will be hit. Again, the reason for moving the 6-3 and 6-4 in this way is that there is really no better alternative. To start your bar with the 6 and to bring another man to the 9 point with the 4 (or to the 10 point with the 3) is a possible alternative, but it is not recommended because we feel it is too much to ask the novice to begin the game in such apparently prodigal fashion. However, once you have learned to play and have acquired some confidence, there is no reason why you should not bring two men down to your bar and your 9 or 10 point with an opening 6-3 or 6-4. This is especially sound when you are the more skillful player, since you are seeking the kind of involvement in which your superior technical skills will weigh most heavily. Conversely, when competing against better players, try to seek simple positions.

The double 4's opening seems so logical that we cannot account for its not having been recommended elsewhere. You will have noticed that we suggest you play opening double 4's and double 3's in much the same way—that is, by establishing one point in your own board and a forward point in your opponent's board. Most experts like making their 9 point and the enemy 5 point with double 4's and two points in their inner board with double 3's. There is nothing *wrong* with these plays, but by playing double 4's and double 3's as we recommend, you have achieved an equilibrium of forces—a balanced position from which it is possible both to attack and to defend—and therefore it seems to us that in total assets, you are distinctly ahead.

An intriguing phenomenon is at work here. When you begin to play backgammon, you are shown the opening positions, the movements of the men are explained, and you are told that the game's object is a race between two opposing armies. Thus, when you have opening rolls of 5-1, 4-1, 2-1, 4-3 or 3-2, your natural first reaction is to play as safely as you can, avoid capture, get around the board, bear off and win. The beginner's instinctive inclination is to think, "Why should I expose a man on my 5 point, which, if hit, will have to go all the way back to the beginning again, whereas if I expose a man in my opponent's inner board by splitting the two back men, it will not cost me nearly so much if hit?"

This argument is spurious, because when such rolls as these five (5-1, 4-1, 2-1, 4-3, 3-2) occur on the opening roll, the game's running element is temporarily suspended in favor of attempting to establish offensive and defensive positions. Should you employ a 1 on the opening roll to start your 5 point and it is hit, no disaster has occurred, but it *might* prove to be disastrous if you split your back men and one or both of them are hit.

There are even certain minor advantages to being hit on your 5 point, since a subsequent roll of 5-4, ordinarily a liability, allows you to make your opponent's 5 point, and subsequent rolls of 4-3, 3-2 and even 2-1 allow you to establish forward positions in your opponent's board. A subsequent roll of double 6's, of course, would be completely wasted, but one cannot expect a panacea.

With an opening roll of 2-1, a possible alternative to our recommended play would be to move one man from your opponent's 12 point to your own 10 point. The movement of the 2-1 is somewhat different from the 5-1 and 4-1, since you can play the 1 in your outer board. With the 5-1 and the 4-1, you are almost forced to start your 5 point, since it is inadvisable to use the 1 in your outer board by dropping it on your bar point, or, in the case of 4-1, to stack more men on your 8 point. To start the bar point is wrong because it is not as valuable as the 5 point; besides, the man exposed on the bar point is more likely to be hit than the exposed man on the 5 point.

In the early stages of the game, the difference in value between the 5 point and the bar point cannot be overemphasized. The most important reason for this is that if you have made the 5 point and your opponent is hit and then rolls any 5, he is necessarily restricted. He must enter with the other number and then play the 5 elsewhere in his board. Had you made the bar point instead, this restriction would not exist. The bar point does block double 6's, but the 5 point blocks double 4's. The advantage of the 5 point over the bar point remains clear-cut. Conversely, if you occupy your opponent's 5 point, he will think twice about bringing blots into his outer board, since they will be in the direct line of your fire.

Backgammon, in fact, is centered around the 5 points. They are the fulcrums around which the game revolves. When your opponent secures one, you must attempt to secure the other. This is the chief reason for dropping a 1 to the 5 point on opening rolls of 5-1, 4-1 and 2-1. Given the great value of the point, it is worth almost any risk to secure it.

These, then, are our suggested opening moves, and we have attempted to present reasonable arguments in favor of each of them. They are fundamental to the playing of the game—first principles, tactical probes of the enemy's position. The object of any opening campaign strategy is to reach a position by disciplined maneuvering in which one army has acquired a tactical advantage over the other. These are the first sure steps in that direction. As soon as you have learned these opening moves, you will know only a small fraction of what you have to know in order to play backgammon well. But it is a start, and an important one. Learn these moves by heart.

Essential Replies to Basic Opening Moves

Following the opening move, backgammon is no longer a game of routine—and having been learned, many basic principles must be temporarily put aside. This becomes immediately apparent when both players have completed their opening moves, and this will be discussed in detail in Chapter Three. When just one player has completed his opening roll, however, and the other player has not yet moved, some of our suggested opening maneuvers have to be altered in order to combat the new position the first player has created in the board.

For example, in Diagram 30, white has played an opening 6-1, and red now rolls double 6's. It would not, as some experts suggest, be advisable to move four men down from white's 12 point to red's bar point. The recommended play is to move two men down from white's 12

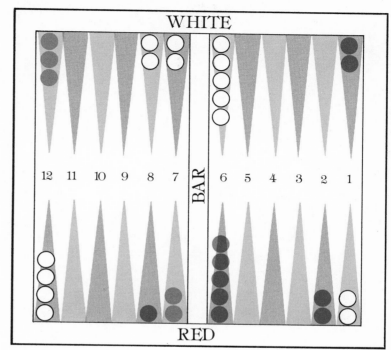

Diagram
30

point to red's bar point, and two men from red's 8 point to red's 2 point. This play prevents red from breaking white's 12 point early in the game—an unusually bad practice.

In Diagram 31, white has again played an opening roll of 6-1 and red now rolls a 6-5. Since white's bar point is blocked, red cannot run one man from white's 1 point out to white's 12 point as he would normally do. It is best, therefore, to move two men down from white's 12 point to red's 8 and bar points. Do not move one man from white's 12 point down to red's 2 point. It accomplishes nothing, and since red must gamble in this situation, it would be best for him to place a blot on his bar point, since it is more valuable to secure if not hit.

When white has opened with a roll of 6-1, most of

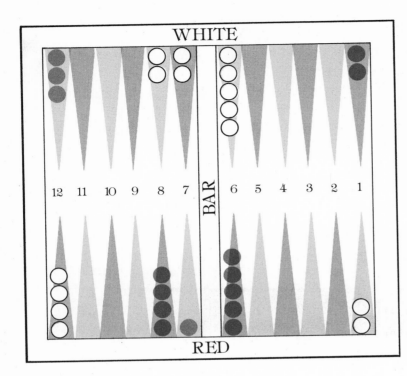

Diagram
31

red's other standard opening replies should be played as suggested earlier. There are those experts who recommend moving the 5-4, the 4-3 and the 3-2 differently—that is, by bringing up one man from white's 1 point before they are hemmed in—but this is a flagrant error. If red ever contemplated such a move, it would be better if he did it *before* white had made his bar point. But either way, it is wrong. His point in white's inner board has now become red's chief defensive block, and it is incorrect to abandon it here. These tactics in no way are cowardly. They are simply common sense, attempting to use what assets red has to best advantage. Never be craven, but don't be foolhardy either.

In Diagram 32, white has completed an opening roll

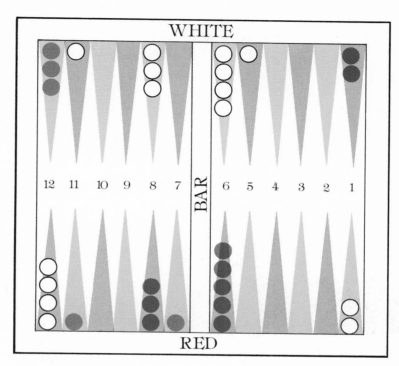

Diagram
32

of 2-1 and red responds with a 6-2. In normal circumstances, we have suggested that red move one man from white's 12 point to his own 5 point. But the circumstances have now changed. In this instance, red's best answer to the 2-1 is to bring two men down from white's 12 point, placing them on his own 11 and bar points. It is a sound offensive play. Red is vulnerable to a direct 6, but white may want to use a 6 to cover his blot on the 5 point. Any 6, 3 or 1 covers this blot, so it would be unwise for red to expose a man to being hit by a 4. *Whenever possible, if you have to leave a blot, try to have it vulnerable to being hit by a number that your opponent could use elsewhere to his advantage.*

In Diagram 33, if white has had an opening roll of 4-

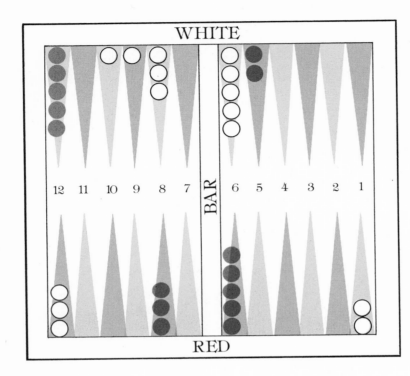

WHITE

12 11 10 9 8 7 | BAR | 6 5 4 3 2 1

RED

Diagram
33

3, red's correct response, should he now roll double 2's, is to bring two men up from white's 1 point to white's 5 point. This is a valuable defensive play and nullifies the threat of white's outer builders. If white had opened with 3-2, 5-2 or 5-4, red would play the double 2's this same way. Under no circumstances should red use the 2's to hit a man in the outer board.

In Diagram 34, white has rolled an opening 6-3, and instead of making our recommended play, has started red's bar point with one man and has moved the other man from red's 12 point to his own 10 point. Red now rolls double 6's. In this instance, it would not be a weak play for red to hit white twice, making his own 1 point. Admittedly, this contradicts not only our suggested opening play for double

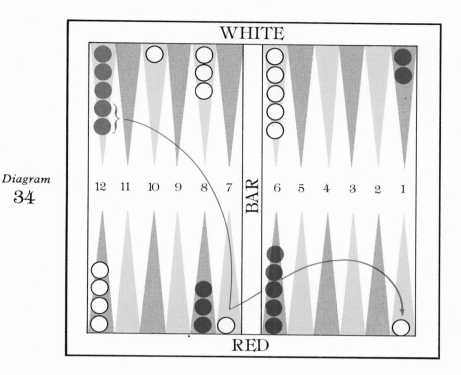

Diagram
34

6's, but also the general rule of never establishing the 1 point early in the game. Nonetheless, red now has two points in his inner board and two of white's men on the bar. Should white now roll a 6 or a 1—and he is a 5 to 4 favorite to do so—thereby bringing only one man back into play, red may be able to blitz him before white can get started again. However, if red is the weaker player, it would be more sensible for him to use his double 6's to make both bar points, as originally recommended.

Again, in Diagram 35, if white has had an opening roll of 6-3 and runs a man from red's 1 point out to red's 10 point, and red now responds with a 6-3, red should hit white's blot and start his own bar point. The same principle would apply if red had rolled a 6-4, except that in this

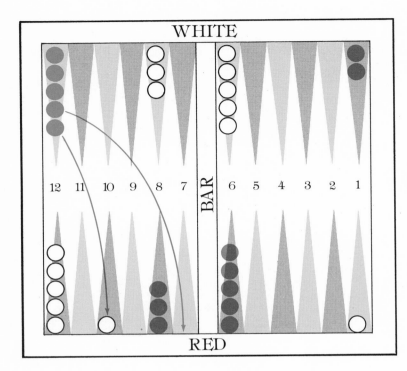

Diagram
35

case, red would start white's bar point in order to combat white's blot. These are dangerous and aggressive counters, but they are recommended.

In Diagram 36, if white has had an opening roll of either 5-1, 4-1 or 2-1, and instead of making our recommended play, moves the 1 from red's 1 point to red's 2 point, and red responds with an opening roll of 4-1, he should, once again, deviate from the suggested opening move. In this case the correct move is to hit white twice by moving a man from red's 6 point to his 1 point. On this specific occasion, 4-1 becomes a reasonably good opening move.

In Diagram 37, if red has an opening roll of 3-1 and

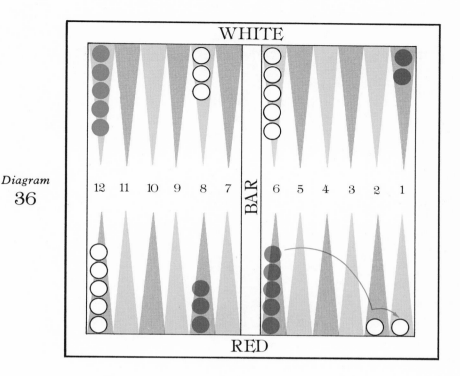

Diagram
36

makes his 5 point, and white responds with 3-2, he should adhere to our recommended opening move. This principle would also apply if he had rolled a 4-3. More than ever, white should be wary of splitting his back men. White's best chance to combat red's initial advantage is to bring two builders into his outer board in order to counterattack. To split inside, thereby weakening his chief defense, is folly, and yet certain experts continue to recommend it.

A good general rule: When in doubt, hit. But there must be a doubt! For example, in Diagram 38, white has opened with a 5-1 and has dropped his 1 onto his 5 point. Red now rolls a 3-1. Ordinarily red would make his 5

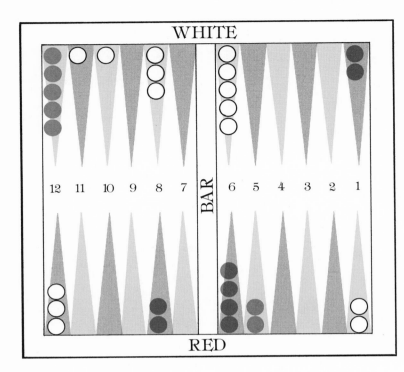

WHITE

| 12 | 11 | 10 | 9 | 8 | 7 | BAR | 6 | 5 | 4 | 3 | 2 | 1 |

RED

Diagram
37

point, but in this case he should hit white's exposed man. In fact, red should do this with any 4 except for double 1's. There is certainly no doubt as to how double 1's should be played.

As must now be apparent, the astute player learns to change or modify even the most routine of moves, even as early as on the opening roll. Other than these important variations, almost all other responses to opening moves should be played in the suggested way — except, of course, when it is possible to hit an exposed man. The most interesting opening variations occur when the player rolling second throws a double. This will be discussed further in

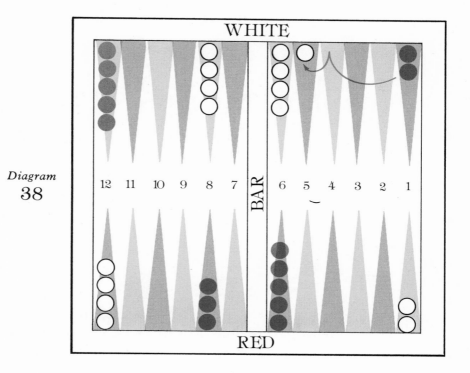

Diagram
38

Chapter Three because these moves are not only interesting, but illustrate how rapidly the game changes shape and direction.

◄3►

THE TACTICS OF THE GAME

Military tactics are the integral means
through which the enemy's destruction or
submission is the ultimate end.

— Karl von Clausewitz

Expressed in its most simple form, the objective of backgammon is for one player to move his men around and off the board before his opponent can do the same. Regardless of what tactics either player employs, this is the game's guiding principle. In order to do this most effectively, the good player learns to establish certain defensive and offensive positions. Thus, the object of the game is to run, but its method is to seek secure and unassailable positions, the most important of which are the two 5 points.

To illustrate this: take the opening rolls of 6-2, 5-1, 4-1 and 2-1. If the sole strategy of the game were to run, each of these rolls would be moved as far as they could go. But this would be a losing proposition, since it would greatly reduce the options of play. However, if these rolls are played correctly, as suggested in Chapter Two, they are employed primarily to seek position. They are little more than minor risks by which the player hopes to acquire major territorial gains.

From the start, there is a complicated interplay of possibilities, probabilities, good fortune and bad, which influences every facet of the game. In backgammon, to seek position is to take certain calculated risks, and because all players are ruled by the dictates of the dice — or by chance, which Karl von Clausewitz, the nineteenth-century military theorist, described as "an agency indifferent to the actor's preference for the outcomes" — no player is ever entirely in control of his particular destiny. One of the game's chief tactics, then, is to shield oneself against the dice. The player with the stronger position can withstand a greater number of unfavorable rolls, or "bad luck," than can the more weakly positioned player, who, because he has failed to protect himself, is more easily assaulted and overrun.

Nonetheless, no matter how cunningly you play, you are virtually always vulnerable. One unexpected horror roll can undermine the best positions and derange the most sensible of plans; this is both the charm and the frustration of the game. The best players of backgammon know that they must employ the craftiest of tactics, not because of the dice, but *in spite of* them. It is the enormously high luck factor in backgammon that causes it to be a game of skill. Without luck or accident, the game would not only be monotonous, but infinitely less skillful.

In backgammon, to be skillful is to be self-protective. At any given point in the game, the better players are aware of Murphy's Law, which states that "If anything can go wrong, it will." Given the whimsical nature of the dice, all players have a chance in the game, but some players have more chances than others because they have created an environment in which the propitious is more likely to occur.

"Running game," then, is a misnomer. Unless both

players throw two consecutive opening 6-5's, the running game in itself is incomprehensible, a contradiction in terms. In backgammon there is no neat and tidy sprint along the flat; the game is more in the nature of a steeplechase and the race is rarely won by the merely swift. The better the player, in fact, the less anxious he is to commit himself to a race. A race is a crap-shoot, and so the better player seeks involvement—conflict with the enemy, in which his superior technical skills will prevail. There must be contact and constant jockeying for position. Developing position is the paramount part of the early game. The first decision as to whether to run or to stay and fight is made on the opening roll and usually will shift and change repeatedly in the course of a single game.

Therefore the accepted notion that backgammon is neatly divided into such concepts as the running game and the blocking game can be dispensed with. To see backgammon in this way is to misunderstand the game's primal strategies. Like chess, backgammon is almost exclusively a game of position. It is no coincidence that chess is played with soldiers and knights, castles and kings. In both theory and practice, chess and backgammon are games of war and depend upon exact and useful strategies.

As has been stated, the basics are relatively simple, but early on you must learn when to make certain moves which are exactly contrary to the basics you have been taught. Some players never grasp this. No sooner does the game start than immediate adjustments must be made because of your opponent's position. For instance, assume that you open with a 6-5 and the enemy counters with 1-1. You now roll 6-1. Hit him instead of making your bar. Here it is only your second roll, and already you are being told to play it in a new manner.

It may help you to overcome these apparent contradictions if you look upon all four segments of the board as a battlefield. You must try to be as strong as possible in every area. If you have an impregnable defense—say, a strong back game—you can become as daring as you wish, leaving blots everywhere. If you have a strong offense—such as having the enemy behind a prime—you can safely weaken your defense. Attempt to establish one or the other, and try not to be weak in both at the same time.

Imagine a general, a Bonaparte, astride his horse on the heights at Austerlitz. It is possible to survey the sweeping moves and countermoves of two opposing armies on the open plain below. Through the use of swift and competent couriers, the general instructs his legions to advance here, to fall back there, to assault, retreat, entrap, to thrust and parry. From his position it is possible to pinpoint the strengths and weaknesses of both factions and to deploy his men accordingly. If he is swifter, craftier, and more ably understands the art of war, this general will, barring untoward accidents, tend to defeat his enemy. These are also the principal tactics of backgammon. The game is conducted from offensive and defensive positions of strength—or apparent strength—employing an intricate blend of pace, balance and power. In short, it is the deft and deceptive art of being in the right place at the right time and knowing how best to take advantage of it.

Try constantly to use your reasoning process. Often the routine move may look good but in reality is weak. Train yourself to anticipate, to realize that should you move one way, it will give the enemy a breathing spell, while another move may let him attack you where you are vulnerable, so that this third and, at first glance, "wrong" choice may be the most intelligent.

All of backgammon's opening moves can be learned by heart, but almost immediately thereafter both sides are involved in the whys and wherefores of the game—often after only the second or third roll. Tactics, then—what the player intends to do in the game and how he intends to control it—become very important at this early juncture. Some of the most interesting variations of early tactics occur when one player throws a double on his opening roll. For instance, in Diagram 39, red has opened with a 4-2 and white has responded with double 4's. Red then rolls a 3-2. Now, red does not want white occupying his 5 point, and so, in order to entice him from that point, he moves a 2 from white's 12 point to his own 11 point, giving white a direct 6 with which to hit him. He plays his 3 from his own 6 point to his 3 point. There are other alternatives, of course, such as moving one man from white's 12 point to red's 8 point, but they are not as satisfactory.

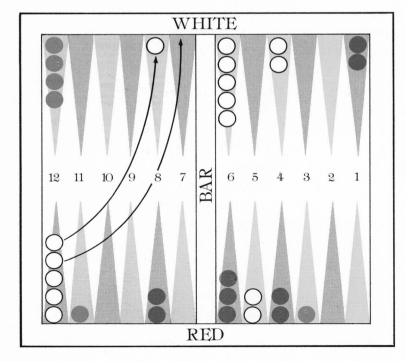

Diagram
39

At this point, white rolls a 6-5, which would appear to be an ideal roll. White can come off the 5 point now and hit red's blot, then continue on to his own 9 point. But this play would be incorrect. The 5 point is white's main defensive bastion and he should not relinquish it lightly. The better play would be to move one man from red's 12 point to white's 8 point and to start white's bar point with the 6.

This is the real beginning of backgammon; the game is no longer being played by rote. The impression of boldness in this play is deceptive; it is merely logical. Consider white's position if red now rolls double 1's or double 3's. To play the 6-5 any other way, white would have too much to lose and too little to gain. If he were race-oriented, as almost all beginners are, hitting and moving on to white's 9 point would be his move, but this is not yet a race and it is a perfect time to leave a blot—especially when there is so much to be gained should red fail to hit it. This is a good example of early imaginative tactical play.

In Diagram 40, white rolls an opening 5-1 and plays it correctly by moving one man from red's 12 point to his own 8 point, and dropping one man from his 6 point to his 5 point. Red then rolls double 4's, moving two men up from white's 1 point to white's 5 point and two men from his own 8 point to his 4 point. Red, of course, hits white's blot on white's 5 point. White now responds with double 1's. He comes in with one man on red's 1 point, and he drops another man from his 8 point to his bar point, but instead of covering it, he moves two men up from red's 1 point to red's 2 point. This move not only threatens red's blot, but gives white a stronger defensive position. To cover the blot on his bar point would be purposeless. White's tactics are to lure red from his 5 point in order to recapture it himself. Red now rolls a 3-1 and makes his

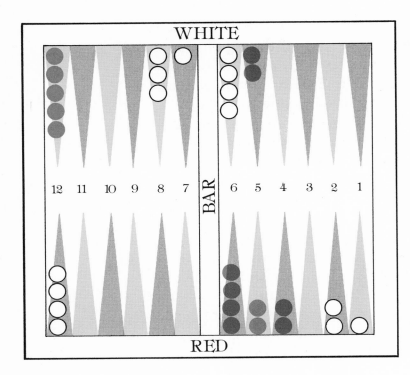

Diagram
40

own 5 point by moving one man in from his 8 point and one man from his 6 point.

White, now in a weakened position, rolls a 6-5. Diagram 41 illustrates the correct way to play the 6-5. White might have covered the blot on his bar point, but again, it would serve little purpose. The vastly superior play is to move two men—one from red's 1 point and another from his 2 point—and establish a point on red's bar point. By doing this, white has exhibited a real grasp of the game. White should make this play under all conditions—in both tournaments and money games. In this instance, red's bar is a stronger tactical position than his own. It is a pertinent example of early tactics and logic, and emphasizes the principle that in the early stages of the game your oppo-

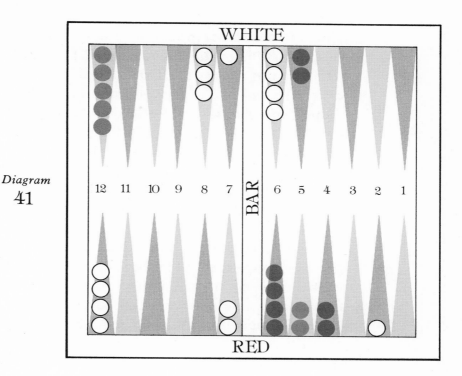

Diagram
41

nent's bar point is more valuable than your own, especially when the enemy holds an advanced point in your board.

The recurring leitmotif in backgammon is the strength or weakness of the two 5 points. In this example, red has secured both of them, and white must do everything in his power to drive his opponent off at least one of them. To play the 6-5 in any other way is not only wrong, it is craven. True, there are disaster rolls for white such as double 2's or double 4's, but he has done the best he can with his dice. More importantly, should those horror rolls *not* occur—and the odds, of course, are against them—white has secured a strong position without having obtained either 5 point.

There are many crucial and constantly recurring situations in which beginners invariably make the wrong tactical plays. One of the most common is that of making your own 1 point too early in the game. The 1 point is often called the *guff* and is derived from the name of a man who, though he otherwise played backgammon well, had an invincible habit of making his 1 point in the beginning stages of the game, or as soon as his opponent vacated the position.

Making the 1 point early on is almost always a weak and worthless play, and as a general rule, it should be avoided. It is the point of no return; if it is made too soon, the men occupying it are out of play for the rest of the game. Moreover, should other points be open in your inner board, when your opponent is picked up and then enters from the bar, he is necessarily advanced. The 1 point is a kind of limbo in which the men imprisoned there must wait till the very end of the game before being borne away to better things.

There is, to be sure, one important exception to this general rule of thumb, which can arise, and often does, at the very start of play. If your opponent, red, has rolled a 6-4, 6-3 or 6-2 and moves one man from your 1 point into your outer board, or if he has split his back men, advancing one man to either your 2 or 3 point, and you then roll double 5's, the 1 point becomes much more attractive. In Diagram 42, you can see that it is now advisable to move two 5's from your 8 point to your 3 point and two 5's from your 6 point to your 1 point. This aggressive tactic has established two immediate points in your inner board and has hit at least one of your opponent's men (if red was foolish enough to leave two blots in your inner board, he now may well have two men on the bar). As can be seen in the diagram, this play has given white three points in his inner board, and if red fails to enter on his next roll, white

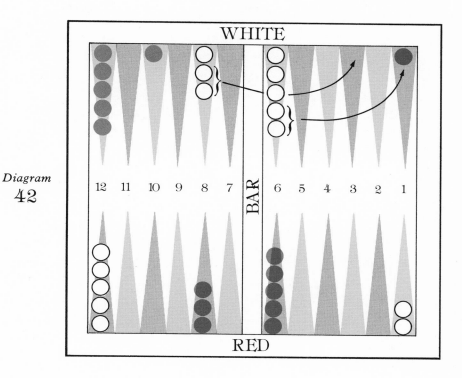

Diagram
42

has an excellent chance to win a double game. This is a good aggressive play and is the only exception to the general rule of not making your 1 point early in the game.

Another example of early tactical play is illustrated in Diagram 43. Red's reply to white's opening 5-1 is double 6's, making both bar points. White then rolls a 4-2, making his 4 point and leaving a blot on his 5 point. Red now rolls a 5-2. (The same general principle applies to rolls of 5-3 and 5-4.) Should red break on this roll—that is, should he move one man from his opponent's bar point to his opponent's 12 point and the other man to his opponent's 9 point? Certain experts have suggested that in the relatively early stages of the game this is a sound and acceptable risk. But this is not entirely true. To begin with,

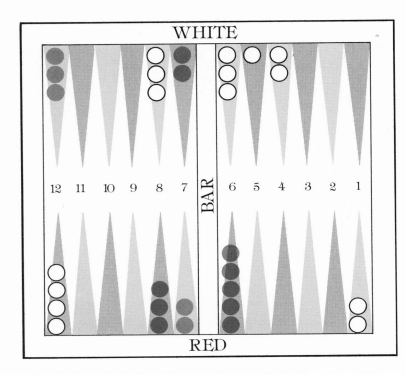

WHITE

12 11 10 9 8 7 BAR 6 5 4 3 2 1

RED

Diagram
43

in the early development of the game, your opponent's bar point is extremely valuable. But there are other considerations. If red is ahead in a race and—more importantly—is the weaker player, it would be sensible to run. Red is a distinct favorite not to be hit (approximately 2¼ to 1 if he rolled a 5-4, 9 to 5 with a 5-3 and 8 to 5 with a 5-2), and should he escape, he has negated white's superior skill. If red is ahead and escapes, he should double or, in a similar position much later in the game, redouble if the doubling block is on his side.★ Every opportunity of this kind should be grasped. White may, in fact, be a very slight underdog in this position, but this is relatively unimportant when

★See Chapter Seven for a discussion of the doubler.

The Tactics of the Game ◄ 61

the game becomes a straightforward game of dice. To fight the superior opponent on his own ground will probably entail complicated technical decisions in which the enemy has had more experience and hence a better chance to win.

These tactical moves apply, however, only when red is the weaker player. If red is the superior player in the above position, and even if he is ahead in a race, it would be folly to move his men from white's bar point. With the 5-2, red should bring a man from white's 12 point to his own 8 point with the 5, and start his 4 point with the 2. With the 5-3, he should make his 3 point with men from his 8 point and his 6 point. With the 5-4, he should move a man from white's 12 point to his own 4 point. You will note that red's blot, left after the 5-2 and the 5-4, can be hit by a 3, but this is not dangerous because, unless white rolls 3's and 1's specifically, he cannot hit red's blot and cover his blot on his own 5 point. Should white roll the perfect shot (hit and cover), it is still no disaster for red; he has three places to come in on his opponent's board (which makes him a 3 to 1 favorite), and he has that fine defensive point on his opponent's bar. The more experienced player always seeks involvement in order to implement his skills. In this position, to risk being hit is to give yourself up to the dice. In tactical plays of this kind, the abilities of your opponent invariably influence your play. What is sound in one situation is madness in another.

Another example of subtle tactical play occurs in Diagram 44. Red has opened with a 4-3, bringing two men down to his 10 and 9 points in attacking positions. White counters with double 2's, but instead of making the recommended opening play, correctly brings two men up from red's 1 point to red's 5 point in order to thwart red's two extra builders. Red then throws double 1's. In this instance, there is little point in red's making his bar point,

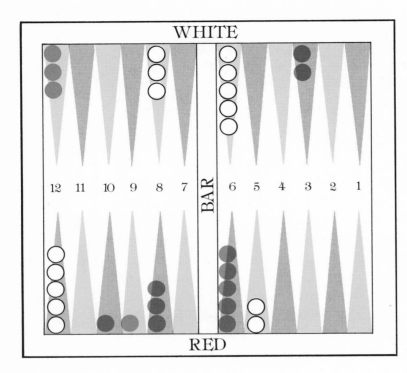

WHITE

12 11 10 9 8 7 BAR 6 5 4 3 2 1

RED

Diagram
44

since white already occupies his 5 point. The sound tactical play in this position is for red to ignore his blots and to move his double 1's from white's 1 point to the 3 point. This is another illustration of a player attempting to lure the enemy off his own valuable 5 point. It is true that red is giving his opponent options, which under normal circumstances he should not do, but in this situation he has little choice. We realize that few players would make this seemingly bold move, but not only is it the more conservative play, it is also correct.

Here again, we can see that on only the third move of the game, one of the players has a vital decision to make, and that this decision, even at this early juncture, could affect the outcome of the game. Learning such early tactics is like learning the alphabet. Once he has learned them, however, the ambitious player must then learn to improvise, to juggle the letters in order to form more difficult and complicated word combinations. The opening moves can be learned by rote; they are routine 99 percent of the time. But immediately thereafter, both opponents become involved in positions in which thought, deduction and the imaginative exercise of tactics are of paramount importance.

At first, such tactics appear more esoteric than they really are, and if the beginner does not grasp their logic right away, he should remember that they can be learned. It is little more than the difference between learning to walk and learning to dance. At some point subsequent to learning the opening steps, a player, if he is to improve, must learn to improvise and perform on his own. He must learn the rules of the game and then deduce how and when to break them, *since backgammon is all too often played in contradiction of its own laws*. Thus, a talent for the game presupposes a certain presence of mind, an imaginative rendering of tactical detail, a knowledge of the specifics of situations. In short, as Clausewitz said of war, "It is the power to discriminate, rather than the readiness to generalize."

◄ 4 ►

BASIC ODDS
AND PROBABILITIES

*All action in war is directed on probable,
not on certain, events.*
—Karl von Clausewitz

A knowledge of the odds
and probabilities is essential to backgammon. They are not
difficult. Most beginners look upon the odds as a kind of
mathematical hocus-pocus and turn away, as from a
strange and somehow frightening fog. But this is usually
because the figures have been presented to them as something complex and difficult to learn. If you are particularly
adept at mathematics, this knowledge will help your game,
but a rudimentary grasp of simple arithmetic is all that is
basically required. Most of the odds and probabilities in
backgammon could be learned in a day by any normally
bright ten-year-old.

Should these assurances be insufficient, we would like
to point out that we know several backgammon enthusi-
asts, some of whom would qualify in the semi-expert class,
who either refuse to learn the odds for the usual obstinate
reasons, or are just too indolent to care. Though their
games would be much improved if they took the time to
learn the percentages, the fact remains that they have

achieved startling success without them. But these are the exceptions; normally, a knowledge of the odds is essential to the game.

The important thing to remember at the start is that these odds are so simple and logical that mathematical misfits have been known to learn them in a surprisingly short time. Ignore the fact that hitherto math has been anathema to you and concentrate briefly on the following paragraphs. We do not intend a complicated lecture; rather, we will direct your mind to the natural logic of the game. Backgammon is basically a game of logic upon logic upon logic, like a series of simple children's blocks.

To begin with, there are two dice for each player. You are concerned with only two at a time, either yours or those of your opponent. Each die has six sides, numbered from 1 through 6.

Now, when rolled, two dice produce any one of only 36 combinations. No more: just 36. Regardless of how many times you roll the dice, you will never roll more than 36 combinations. You would agree that this limits the study considerably. What are these 36 combinations? If the dice show any specific double—as, for example, a 2 and a 2—this is one of the 36 combinations. Therefore, rolls of 1-1, 2-2, 3-3, 4-4, 5-5 and 6-6, the only possible doubles, account for 6 of the possible 36 combinations, leaving 30 others. If any two different numbers appear when the dice have been rolled—a 2 and a 1, for example—this roll will account for 2 combinations. Why 2? Well, a 2 on one die and a 1 on the other is one combination. But would it not have been possible for the 2 to have been a 1 and the 1 to have been a 2? Since both of these combinations must be included, whenever you roll two different numbers they count as two different combinations. Therefore, adding up all of your possible rolls—excluding, for the moment, doubles — you would have the following combinations:

1-2	2-1
1-3	3-1
1-4	4-1
1-5	5-1
1-6	6-1
2-3	3-2
2-4	4-2
2-5	5-2
2-6	6-2
3-4	4-3
3-5	5-3
3-6	6-3
4-5	5-4
4-6	6-4
5-6	6-5

Note that the sum total of these is 30, which, added to the 6 doubles, makes a grand total of 36 different possible combinations of the dice.

Now, if 1-1 has one chance out of 36 of being thrown, how many other rolls are there that might have appeared? The answer, of course, is 35. Thus, since there is only one 1-1 and 35 other possible combinations, is it not logical and ridiculously transparent that the odds against rolling a 1-1 on any and all individual rolls are 35 to 1?

We have pointed out that any number which is not a double constitutes 2 combinations. What, then, are the odds against rolling a 6-5? There are 2 combinations that produce the 6-5 (6 on one die and 5 on the other, or 5 on the first die and 6 on the second), and 34 that do not (since the 2 combinations subtracted from the 36 possible rolls are 34). When reduced to its lowest common denominator, the fraction $^{34}/_2$ is $^{17}/_1$, so the odds against rolling a 6-5 on any specific roll are exactly 17 to 1. (Incidentally, if you have ever visited the Las Vegas casinos in order to play craps, you may recall that they will offer you only 14 to 1 on exactly the same proposition, one of the several reasons they are unlikely to go broke.)

Now the first key formula is established. A roll of 1-1 has been shown to be a 35 to 1 shot and 6-5 a 17 to 1 shot. *You now know the exact odds of every combination that two dice can possibly show.* Not only double 1's but all other specific doubles are 35 to 1, and not only 6-5 but all other combinations, excluding doubles, are 17 to 1.

As mentioned in Chapter Two, the most often used fraction in backgammon is 25 to 11. Try to remember this despite the fact that it seems an odd, lopsided number. Why 25 to 11? You are already equipped to understand the answer.

This figure represents the exact odds against you when you have a single shot at one of your opponent's blots. For instance, let us assume that your opponent is bearing off and has a closed board except for a blot on his 4 point. You are on the bar, and only a roll of a direct 4 by you can hit it. How many of the 36 combinations on the dice will produce the 4?

$$
\begin{array}{ll}
 & 4\text{-}4 = 1 \\
4\text{-}1 & 1\text{-}4 = 2 \\
4\text{-}2 & 2\text{-}4 = 2 \\
4\text{-}3 & 3\text{-}4 = 2 \\
4\text{-}5 & 5\text{-}4 = 2 \\
4\text{-}6 & 6\text{-}4 = \underline{2} \\
 & \phantom{6\text{-}4 = } 11
\end{array}
$$

Eleven rolls will hit your opponent's blot, and the remaining 25 rolls will not. Thus, the odds against your rolling a 4 are 25 to 11. Extending this formula, the odds against rolling any specific number are again exactly 25 to 11.

Try to grasp the logic behind these basic computations. If you do understand everything we have discussed so far in this chapter, you are well on your way to learning virtually all you need to know about the purely mathematical aspects of backgammon. Of course, the game is much more than plain numbers, but here we are interested specifically in basic percentages and probabilities.

You now know that *any* time you have one direct shot at one of your adversary's open men, regardless of what that shot is—a 1, 2, 3, 4, 5, or 6—you are a 25 to 11 underdog. That is, he is approximately a 2¼ to 1 favorite not to be hit. But now let us assume you have a 4 to hit and there are no intervening checkers between your man and his. Are you able to calculate your exact chances of hitting? Since you have the tools, try to work it out before reading further. But do not be dismayed if you fail; it cannot be reiterated often enough how comparatively simple this whole chapter will become when you have thought it through.

You have already learned that there are 11 chances to roll a direct 4. To that you must add those numbers that total 4 on *both* dice; these are 1-1, 2-2 and 3-1. Since 3-1 comprises two shots and 1-1 and 2-2 are one apiece, there are a total of four extra chances, which you must add to the original 11—making a total of 15 chances. If 15 rolls hit, how many miss? Subtracting 15 from 36 (the total number of combinations), you get 21. The odds, then, against you are now 21 to 15, or exactly 7 to 5, which is much better for you than 25 to 11.

Assume that you have one direct shot, which as you know by now makes you a 25 to 11 underdog. The percentage figure here is 30.55. This is determined by taking the favorable chances—11—and dividing them by the total number of rolls: 36. If you are a 25 to 11 underdog, you will hit 11 times and miss 25 in 36 games over the long run— or, put another way, you will hit 30.55 times and miss 69.45 in 100 games over the long run. Any percentage figure can be determined in this way. If you are a 3 to 1 underdog on a specific roll—there are 27 chances against you to 9 in your favor—you can discover the percentage figure by dividing 36 (the total number of rolls) into 9 (your favorable rolls); the result is 25 percent, or one chance in four—which is to say, 3 to 1. You will hit 9 and miss 27 out of 36, or hit 25 and miss 75 out of 100 if you are a 3 to 1 underdog. These "percentage" figures seem superfluous to us, but are mentioned here in case the reader finds them easier to comprehend.

You can always work out this kind of problem right at the table. You need only to count accurately, and when the options arise, make sure that the percentages work in your favor and not in that of your opponent. It goes without saying that the more often you calculate these percentages, the easier it will become. If you are comparatively new to backgammon and never have been much interested in odds, you now have all the information you require to select the best percentage move. Take your time, count up the shots, compare your choice with your alternatives and then make the play that is most in your favor.

Superstition and hunches play a large part in crucial backgammon decisions. This is all right as far as it goes and is not entirely to be sneered at, but be sure you don't let your superstitious whims defy percentages. Assume, for example, that you have arrived at a critical position in which you are forced to leave a blot, and it is vital for you not to be hit because your opponent has a closed board. Assume also that you have a choice of leaving your blot where it can be hit by a 1 or by a 6, including all the combinations (2-2, 3-3, 4-2, 5-1) because no men intervene. You have a strong feeling that your opponent is going to throw a 1 on his next roll, and your hunch shrieks, "Don't leave him the 1!" Yet there would be grounds for having you committed if you followed this whim and left your man open to being hit by the 6 instead of the 1.

Follow these intuitions only if they are even or better percentage plays than any alternative. Never follow them in defiance of the odds, no matter how strongly you feel.

When any decision has to be made, always attempt to eliminate the guess. A simple, workable formula to apply is to play percentages at all times and to follow whatever hunches occur to you only when the odds are precisely even. A simple, logical approach to backgammon does not mean that you will always win, but you will lose less often.

When you are on the bar, the chances of entering your opponent's board are the other important fundamental odds of backgammon. When you are on the bar and your opponent has a one-point board—probably his 6 point—the only roll on which you cannot enter is a 6-6. Whenever your opponent has a one-point board, you are a 35 to 1 favorite to come in. But should he make just one more point—any point—the odds are reduced to 8 to 1. The explanation is relatively simple. Suppose your adversary has his 6 point to begin with and a short time later also makes his 5 point. Now 6-6, 5-5 and 6-5 (which, as noted earlier, also counts as 5-6)—that is, a total of four shots— will block you from entering. Four shots are bad for you and therefore 32 are good, so the odds are 32 to 4, or 8 to 1, in your favor.

If three points are covered, the odds against you are naturally reduced further; they are now only 3 to 1 in your favor. And if four points are covered, they are reduced still further to only 5 to 4 in your favor. When your opponent has established five points in his board, you are for the first time a distinct underdog, in this case, 25 to 11 against.

The important thing to remember about this is that you must learn not to be frightened of your opponent's board, since it is only when he has established five points that you become an underdog to come in. It is also something of a consolation to know that even if he has established a five-point board, you are still a very slight favorite to enter in two rolls. What is called *entry failure* is a niggling annoyance for everyone. But the next time you are on the bar bemoaning your fate, remember that you are always a favorite to come in unless your opponent has a five-point board, and even then you are a slight favorite to enter in two rolls.

In essence, these are the basic odds of backgammon, and as you have seen, they are neither complicated nor shrouded in that impenetrable fog. If you will spend a little time to master the figures discussed in this chapter, you will be equipped to handle virtually all the problems of the game's percentages.

This subject has been simplified intentionally. It would have been possible to delve more deeply, to discuss the subject in terms of higher equations and negative probabilities, but this kind of approach is unnecessary. In bridge, for instance, if a player is well versed in the fundamentals of the game but has never learned how to bring about a crisscross squeeze, his game is only minimally affected because the odds are that it will come up only once or twice in a lifetime. Similarly, in backgammon you now have all the basic mathematics you need in order to play the game well.

The Odds on Rolling Unobstructed Numbers

1: 25 – 11 against
2: 2 – 1 against
3: 11 – 7 against
4: 7 – 5 against
5: 7 – 5 against
6: 19 – 17 against
7: 5 – 1 against
8: 5 – 1 against
9: 31 – 5 against
10: 11 – 1 against
11: 17 – 1 against
12: 11 – 1 against

The Odds on Entering When a Man Is on the Bar

With a five-point board: 25 – 11 against.
With a four-point board: 5 – 4 in favor.
With a three-point board: 3 – 1 in favor.
With a two-point board: 8 – 1 in favor.
With a one-point board: 35 – 1 in favor.

◄5►

BEARING OFF

The Policy employed in waging war
troubles itself little about final
possibilities, but confines its attention
to immediate probabilities.
—*Karl von Clausewitz*

Bearing off is a science in itself and worth more than the casual study that players normally devote to it. As explained in Chapter One, when any of the points in your inner board are held by your opponent or when any of his men are on the bar, the object is to bear off your men with a combination of speed and safety.

Let us assume that white has a closed board, and that red has a reasonably good inner board and a man on the bar. The optimum position for white is shown in Diagram 45. Of course, the problem is different when your opponent occupies any of your points—that is, bearing off is more difficult—but let us first examine the less difficult position.

In this optimum position, white is a strong favorite not to give a shot—that is, to bear off his men without leaving a blot. As he bears off, he continually attempts to keep his high men even. For example, should white have three men on his 6 point and two men on his 5 point, a roll of double 6's or double 5's or 6-5 would leave a man exposed. This kind of position should be avoided whenever possible. In such situations, your critical point is always your highest point or two points, and you should strive to keep it or them even.

Given white's optimum position in Diagram 45, bearing off is a relatively uncomplicated procedure — though even here it is never certain that you will not leave a blot. Still, it is the safest position at which to aim when bringing men into your inner board prior to bearing off.

The possibilities of being hit increase, of course, when red has established positions on any of white's points in white's inner board. In such an event white's tactics will change — in some cases, deliberately violating the basic rules of bearing off. For instance, in Diagram 46, where white occupies red's 1 point, red has already borne

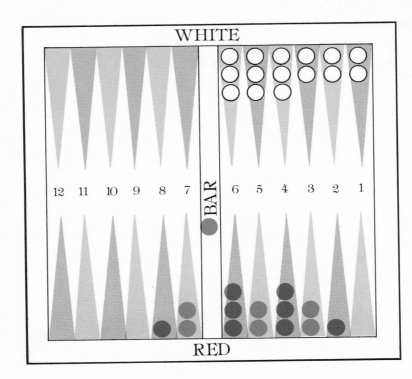

WHITE

12 11 10 9 8 7 BAR 6 5 4 3 2 1

Diagram
45

RED

off three men and has a 1 to play. If red moves his 1 from his 5 point to his 4 point, subsequent rolls of double 4's or a 5-4 will leave a single shot (blot), and the horror roll of 6-5 will leave a double shot. If, however, red moves his 1 from his 3 point to his 2 point, he has broken the cardinal rule of keeping his high men even and has made himself vulnerable to the potentially disastrous rolls of 6-5, 5-4, 5-3, 5-1 and double 6's, or four extra single shots, but no double shots. Which is correct? Against White's prime we would move down from the 5 to the 4 point, risking a double shot. But were White's board no threat, play from the 3 to the 2 point, guaranteeing not to leave two men vulnerable. If red had had a closed board with white on the bar, there would be no question about his moving his 1

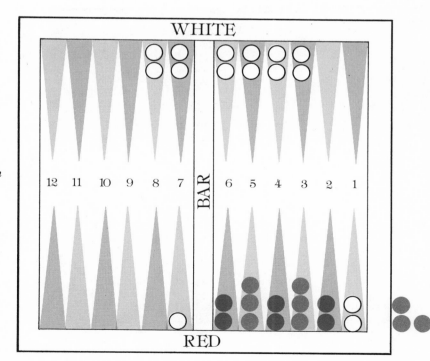

Diagram 46

from the 5 point to the 4 point, since there would be no number that could hurt him in this position. To repeat: your options of play are always dictated by your opponent's position.

Diagram 47 illustrates an example of play in bearing off that seems to contradict all the percentages. White has a closed board and red, who has already borne off five men, now rolls a 5-3. If played strictly according to the percentages, the correct and apparently reasonable play would be to bear off one man from the 5 point and move the other man down to red's 2 point, thereby giving white only a one-shot, the odds of which are 25 to 11 against. In order not to be hit, this in fact is the correct percentage play. On closer examination, however, there is more to this position

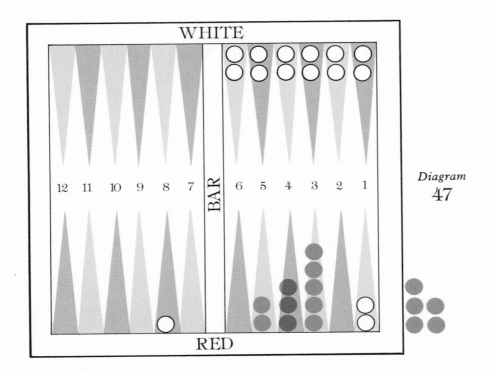

Diagram
47

than percentages. If he is not hit, red's next roll is fraught with danger. Any high number which is not a double, such as 6-5, 6-4 and 5-4, will give a double shot. Double 3's also will give a double shot, and any roll that does not include a 1 or a 2 will leave at least a single shot. The recommended play, therefore, is for red to bear off two men — one from the 5 point and another from the 3 point. By doing this, red is taking a calculated risk. In addition to the direct 4, this gives white two other shots (3-1 and 1-3) at red's blot on the 5 point — odds of 23 to 13 against, but better than 25 to 11. Taking two men off, moreover, gives red seven men off altogether, bringing him to just below the *break-even point* of nine men off. (For an explanation of the break-even point, see p. 83.) But the main reason for making this play is that if red is not hit, his next roll has many more chances of being safe , for regardless of what he rolls, he cannot leave a double shot; thus, it is the better play.

This is a good illustration of fluid reasoning. A good general principle to follow is that if you must leave a blot which, if hit, could cost you the game, it is best to leave it where, according to the percentages, your opponent is least likely to hit it. Yet because of other attendant factors, it is best to contradict the principle in this particular position.

In Diagram 48, white, who has no men off the board, rolls a 5-4. He bears off his 5 and now has an option of playing one of two 4's. There is only one correct way of playing this move. If white takes a man off the 4 point, he can be hit with a 4 or a 3. If he moves a man from his 6 point to his 2 point, he can be hit with a 4 or a 5. In each case, the odds of being hit are exactly the same: red is a 5 to 4 favorite to hit. But if white plays the move correctly — by moving a man down from the 6 point — and red then fails to hit him, on white's next roll he is a solid 8 to 1

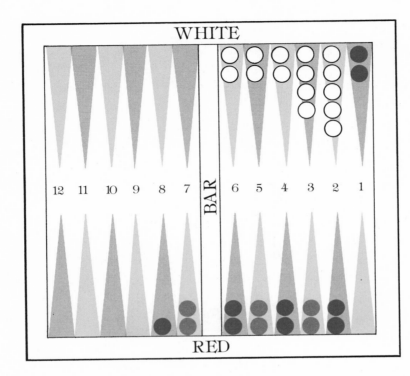

Diagram
48

favorite not to leave a blot. The only bad shots are double 5's and 4's, and 5-1. Had white played his 5-4 the other way—by taking two men off—there would have been 17 rolls which left blots, and in some cases two of them. White would now be only a 19 to 17 favorite not to leave a blot—much less than 8 to 1. The principle involved here is always to leave your blot high up rather than in the middle of your board if possible. If you are not hit, your next roll will be easier to play.

Diagram 49 is an example of a principle that many players, particularly beginners, tend to forget. In this position white, with four men off, has rolled a 5-2. Many new players would move the 5 from the 6 point, hitting red on the 1 point and move a 2 from the 4 point to the 2 point.

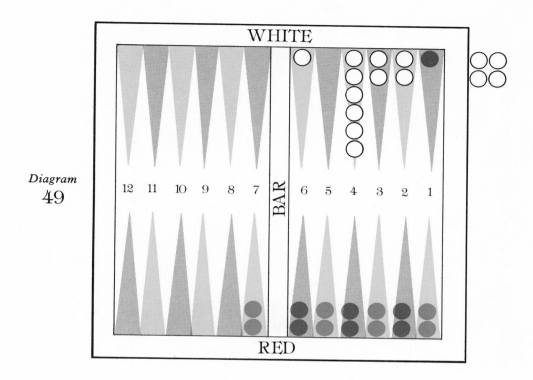

Diagram 49

They forget that the roll can be played in two ways; either number may be played first. Thus, the correct tactic is to move the 2 from the 6 point to the 4 point and then to take off the 5. Playing a 2-5 when bearing off in this position saves white from leaving an unnecessary and dangerous blot.

Again, a paradox. One might easily believe that this principle always applies, but in the following instance, in Diagram 50, it is again more advantageous for white to break the rule. In this position, white has four men off and now rolls a 6-1. The 6-1 should be played by bearing off the 6 and moving the 1 from the 4 point to the 3 point. If he makes the recommended move, white's bad subsequent rolls are double 6's, double 5's and double 4's. But if he

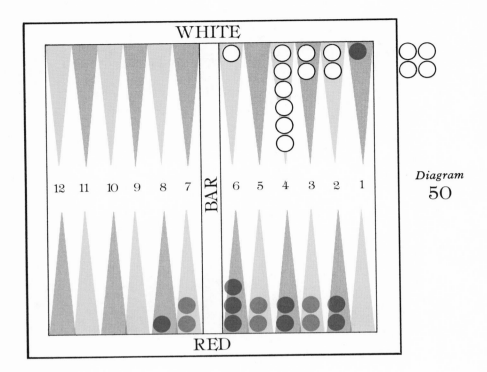

Diagram
50

simply takes the man off the 6 point and leaves six men on his 4 point, he will be vulnerable to a 6-3, 5-3, 4-3 or 2-3, so he will have eight potential bad rolls instead of three. Furthermore, should the horror roll occur—that is, double 6's, double 5's or double 4's—white will still have nine men off, and if his blot is missed, his double-game potential is strong.

In Diagram 51, white has borne off four men and now rolls a 4-3. In this case, white is going all out for a double game. Red is a 5 to 4 favorite to come in. White gains virtually nothing by bearing off two men in this position. He should take a man off the 4 point and move the odd man on the 4 point down to the 1 point. It is safer, and it

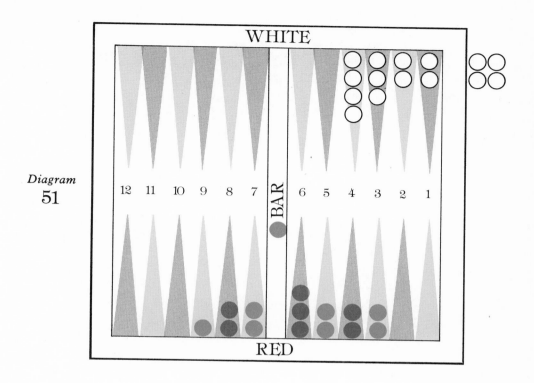

Diagram
51

will still take him the same number of rolls to bear off all his men. (We are assuming, of course, that no doubles will be thrown.) Only double 3's, double 4's, double 5's and double 6's hurt him; even if he rolls them, he will have nine men off and consequently will still be a favorite to win if red hits his blot. Of these doubles, incidentally, double 3's are the worst, since, if white plays them correctly—that is, as safely as possible—he can bear only two men off.

In Diagram 52, red has borne twelve men off and white now rolls a 6-1. Here again, the correct play is to contradict all our principles and to bear one man off the 6 point and another off the 1 point, leaving two blots. It is

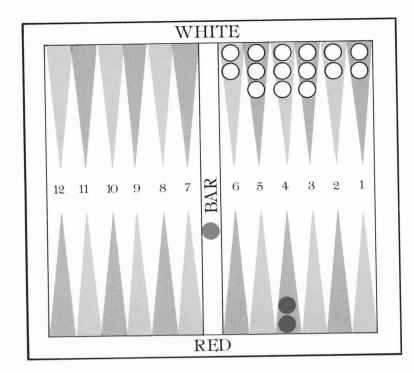

Diagram
52

not played this way because white *wants* to be hit. It is just that it is very much to white's advantage to be hit *if* red rolls a 6 or a 1. Were the blot on the 6 point not there, and red rolled a 6, the game would be virtually over, since red would be a prohibitive favorite in this position. But if the blot on the 6 point is hit, white has an additional opportunity of coming in and hitting red again as he comes around to his home board. More importantly, if red now rolls a 1 without an accompanying 4 or 5 or 6, he will have to break his position in his inner board with any 1, 2 or 3, thereby giving white the unexpected opportunity of being able to capture all three of red's men and winning the game easily. Lastly, if red fails to roll either a 6 or a 1, then white is two men nearer victory.

This is one more example of your opponent's position forcing you into contradicting all the principles you have hitherto learned. It is a position which demands the desperate gamble, since without it all will be lost anyway.

A few basic percentages: If white, against red's closed board, is hit while bearing off, the *break-even point* in terms of his winning is somewhere between eight and nine men off. In other words, when white has borne off nine men, he is a slight favorite to win, but with only eight men off, he is a slight underdog. However, we would recommend that white accept a double⋆ if he has borne off at least six men, provided that all the rest of his men are positioned on his lower points. This recommendation is made on the premise, explored later, that if you are a less than 3 to 1 underdog, in the long run you will gain by accepting the double. If white has borne off all his men but two, and they are on the bar, he may also accept a double, since he is certainly less than a 3 to 1 underdog.

When bearing off, if red, for example, has a closed board and white has borne off all his men except one which is on the bar, white is between a 13- and 14-to-1 favorite to win.

Further, when red has a closed board and is attempting to win a double game, he should not pick up too many of his opponent's men along the way. A safe number of men to capture would be four. This is an important safety factor. The more men white has on the bar, the longer it will take him to come in, and hence the more chances he will have of hitting red while red is bearing off.

The preparation of your board for bearing off—that is, the immediate positioning of your men just prior to bear-

⋆See Chapter Seven on the doubler.

ing off—involves tactics of some importance. It has been suggested by certain experts that in a race you must get your men into your home board as quickly as possible in order to bear off more rapidly. Generally this is true, but since backgammon is replete with sly paradoxes, there are occasions when it is not, and to operate on that principle all the time would be costly. For example, in Diagram 53, red rolls double 1's. In this instance it would be folly to use the double 1's to bring the lone outside man into red's inner board. The correct play is to move two men from the 6 point to the 5 point, one man from the 4 point to the 3 point and one man from the 2 point to the 1 point. Red is still behind, but his position is considerably improved. By

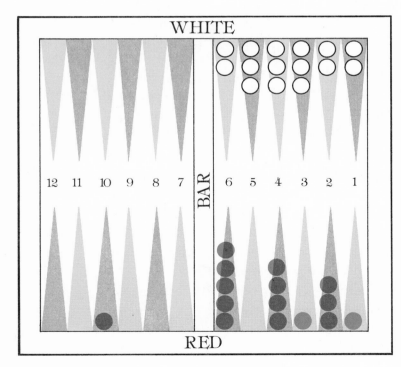

Diagram
53

bringing the one man in, on the other hand, red would, when bearing off, be wasting all rolls of 5's and most rolls of 3's and 1's, and would fall even further behind. To make the point more pragmatically, if red were to bring the lone man in and white then doubled, it would be an almost impossible *take* (acceptance of the double); played the recommended way, if white doubles, red should take it.

A further guideline about coming in: generally speaking, it is wiser to start the high points rather than the low points in your inner board. The only time to start the low points is for diversification, when you have made the high ones already. In a race, when coming in, try not to leave gaps in your inner board. As discussed above, it is usually a good practice to employ 1's for this purpose rather than to advance your outside men.

In Diagram 54, white has borne off twelve men. Red has a 1 to play and is trying to save (avoid losing) a double game. Sometimes the playing of a simple 1 is essential to one's basic strategy, though many players seem to feel that because the roll moves so short a distance and wields no apparent power, it is unimportant. Nothing could be further from the truth. The example shown in Diagram 54 is indicative of this. By playing the 1 correctly here, red increases his chances of saving the double game by exactly 100 percent. It is a good example of how subtle the playing of 1's can be and how careless play can penalize the unobservant player. Many players, nearly resigned to losing the double game and believing the movement of the 1 to be relatively unimportant, would move it from white's 10 point to the 11 point in order to move that much closer home. But by so doing, they have limited themselves to only two rolls that could save them: double 4's and double 6's, a 17 to 1 shot. Had they left the outside man where it

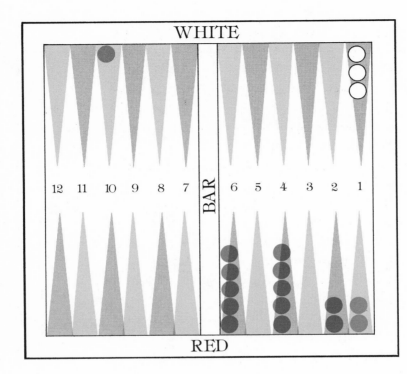

Diagram
54

was, however, and moved a 1 from red's 4 point to the 3 point, double 5's and double 3's would also have saved the double game. Red would now be only an 8 to 1 underdog—assuming, of course, that white did not throw a double himself. As is evident from this and countless other examples, the deployment of 1's can be crucial in general overall tactics.

Diagram 55 is another example of the important use of the 1. In this instance red has a 1 to play before white rolls. Here again the 1 is enormously important. Assuming again that white will not roll a double, if red moves his 1 from the 6 point to the 5 point, he becomes a 19 to 17 favorite to bear both men off on his next roll (there are 19

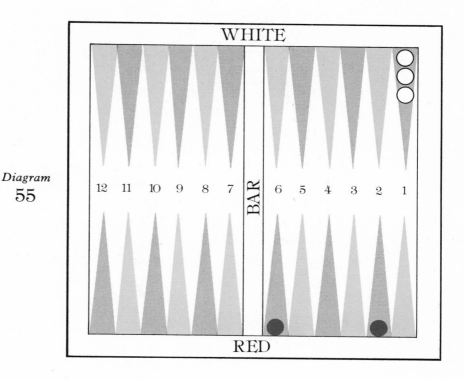

Diagram
55

combinations which will bear off a 5-2). But if he moves the 1 from the 2 point to the 1 point, he will be a 21 to 15 underdog to bear both men off (there are only 15 combinations which will bear off a 6-1).

If a bookmaker could get 19 to 17 on one side of a proposition and 7 to 5 (the same as 21 to 15) on the other, he could retire within a month. This situation actually occurred in a tournament: a player moved the 1 from his 2 point to his 1 point, and when his adversary had completed his next roll, bearing two men off, red then rolled a 6-1 to win the game. His adversary was justifiably perturbed, though he refrained from saying so. A roll of large doubles by red would have been less disturbing, since doubles are built into the game, but to make the wrong move and then throw the perfect number to win is a flagrant example of why backgammon is the cruelest game. Red won *because* he had made the wrong move, and because he won, he believed it was the right move, and it is doubtful that anyone could have persuaded him otherwise.

In Diagram 56, white has already borne off five men and now rolls a 2-1. In this instance, two men should be taken off. Red is a 3 to 1 favorite to come off the bar. By bearing two men off, white saves an entire turn because he has an even number of men left. It is well worth the risk. Bear one man off the 2 point and another off the 1 point. This contradicts the rule of keeping the high men even, but increases white's chances of winning a double game,

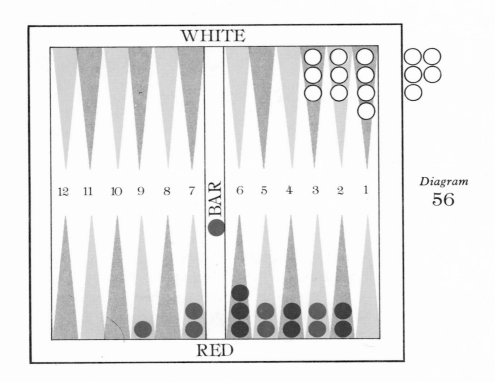

Diagram
56

and at this moment—before he has rolled—red is more than a 17 to 1 underdog to hit.

In Diagram 57, the position is only slightly changed. White has one more man on his 1 point, but because of this, white's strategy also changes. Here white has nothing to gain by taking two men off, as he did in the previous diagram. By doing so, he leaves himself in a position of maximum exposure without having achieved any tangible rewards. In this instance, white should bear off one man from the 3 point. Admittedly, he is still open to being hit if red fails to come in and he then rolls any double except double 1's. Even so, at the moment, it is over 90 to 1 against red hitting white; even if he does, white will have borne off a minimum of seven men (if he rolled double 2's)

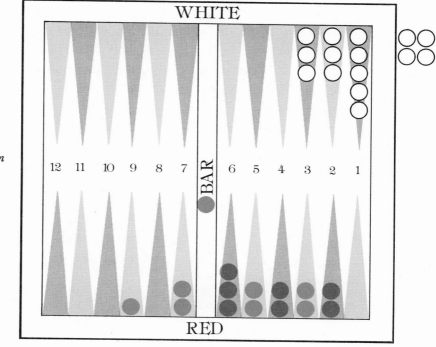

Diagram
57

and with any larger double, he will have borne off nine men.

Unlike the play in Diagram 56, white should not take two men off in this position. We do not object to bold, courageous play; we do deplore plays that make no sense. Bearing two men off does not improve white's position in any way. The reason for the difference between the two plays is one of simple mathematics. If white had taken two men off in this position, he would have created 20 extra chances to leave a blot on his next roll, and if red failed to enter he would have been offered a gratuitous opportunity to hit and win the game. White would have gambled foolishly because he had nothing to gain. To take it a step further, if white had had a mathematical certainty of winning a double game—if, say, red had six men in his outer board instead of three—the obvious correct play would be to play it perfectly safe and move a man from the 3 point and a man from the 2 point down to the 1 point. Again, white's play is influenced by his opponent's position.

Here, as in all other aspects of the game, success is predicated on sound deductive reasoning. We cannot advocate strongly enough that the player think rather than simply push his men about the board. Backgammon is a game of calculated risks. By bearing men off in the recommended way, you have risked a subsequent horror roll of doubles. Why? To hurt yourself? No; because it improves your position. You leave a blot intentionally. Why? Because you have calculated that the potential rewards are worth the risk and that you stand to gain much more than you will lose. This is the essence of backgammon: the ability to assess the different and sometimes difficult choices confronting you.

THE BACK GAME

Defense in itself is a negative exercise,
since it concentrates on resisting the
intentions of the enemy rather than being
occupied with our own.
— *Karl von Clausewitz*

The first general and important axiom concerning back games is that they should be avoided. More often than not, the back game is a rearguard action thrown up to resist the inevitable flood. It can be a colorful and exciting tactical play; it can be brilliantly executed and even rewarding, but in the main, the back game has too many sudden pitfalls, too many built-in snares, to be viable more than half of the time. To begin with, the back game requires meticulous timing and is comparatively easy to defend against by an experienced player; and when disaster strikes, as it is wont to do, even the expert is vulnerable to losing a double or even a triple game. (In England, the back game has a better winning percentage, since triple games are not recognized there.) The timing is so critical that if certain horror numbers are rolled, they can destroy the back game completely. The back game is not a happy place in which to find yourself, and its devotees are reminiscent of the little Dutch boy with his finger in the dike.

If you must play a back game, however—and often

there is little other choice—the principal tactic is to establish at least two fortified positions in your opponent's inner board. To occupy points in your opponent's board is tantamount to invasion, an occupation of enemy territory, not with a view to keeping it, but as Clausewitz said of occupied enemy territory, "in order to levy contributions on it." The preferred points to occupy are the low ones— the 1 and 2 points, the 2 and 3 points or the 1 and 3 points. The 1 and 2 points are the ideal theoretical pair, but only if you have perfect timing. However, it is almost always difficult to time your game perfectly, and in practice the occupation of these two points also tends to stop the enemy from playing 5's and 6's as he is bringing his men in. It is better, therefore, to attempt to establish the 2 and 3 points, or, failing that, the 1 and 3 points.

Having accomplished this, it is to your advantage to have as many of your men hit as possible. This is particularly true if you have established three points in your opponent's inner board. In such a case it would be to your advantage to have all fifteen of your men distributed on these three points. Your opponent would be unable to complete his board and none of your men would be out of play or in any danger of it.

Meanwhile, in your own inner board, you must never attempt to establish forward points—that is, the lower points. They are ineffectual and out of the action. It is much like establishing a forward position when the real war is being waged behind you. Above all, it is important to establish the higher points in your own board, maintaining other men behind them as a kind of mobile reserve in order to make up the rest of your board effectively.

In its essence, the back game is backgammon played in reverse. It is a series of tactical maneuvers which go against all the player's natural aggressive instincts. It is a game in which the defender prefers to be hit and hopes for low numbers rather than high. It is a game for masochists.

The back game can occur quite accidentally right at the outset. In Diagram 58, for example, red had an opening roll of 4-1 and played one man from white's 12 point to his own 9 point, and dropped one man from his 6 point to his 5 point. White responded with double 4's; using one man from red's 1 point he hit red twice, and with two men from his 8 point he established his own 4 point. Red then rolled double 3's, a great shot, entering two men and making his own 5 point, and, as illustrated in the diagram, after only three rolls finds himself immersed in the entanglements of a back game. Like a man suddenly set upon by a dog, red's tactics are now almost exclusively defensive.

In defending a back game, you must try not to help your opponent by hitting his open men. More importantly,

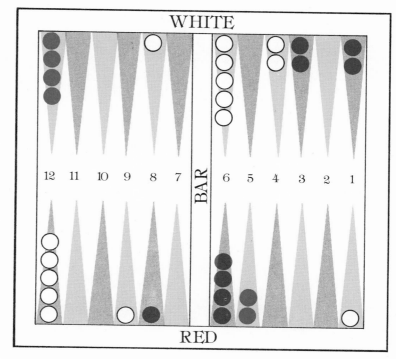

Diagram 58

and particularly if his timing is right, you must allow yourself to be hit, especially when he has no blots in his board. He will attempt to leave as many blots there as possible, since, if you are hit, you may be forced to hit him again, thereby giving him another man in your inner board. Allowing your own men to be hit gives you the necessary delay and may destroy his timing. But this is a matter of some cunning and tactical maneuvering.

Some of these principles are illustrated in Diagram 59. In this position, red rolls a 6-3. Most players in this situation would move their man on white's 5 point out to white's 11 point and move the odd man on their own 10 point to their bar. This illustrates the difficulty of learning the theory inherent in the back game. The play that should be made is to slot the man on white's 10 point on red's 9

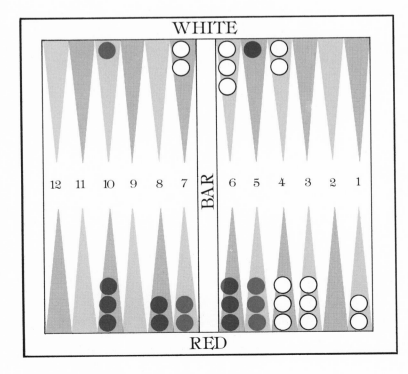

Diagram 59

point, and to move the man on white's 5 point out to white's 8 point. The reasoning behind this tactic is as follows: If white does not roll a 5 or a 6 on his next roll and does not hit your blot, he will have to move forward in his inner board, which he would prefer not to do. Then if red rolls a 1 or an 8 on the next roll, he can cover his open man, thereby restricting white's movements to his own inner board and probably destroying it. On the other hand, if white does roll a 5 or a 6 and hits red, this will give red more time in which to preserve his semi-prime. This is a battle of masochists, since both red and white long to be hit in order to be delayed for as long as possible. White has a beautifully balanced back game, but ultimately he will have to break his anchors on red's 3 and 4 points or destroy his inner board. Red has a fine semi-prime and should strive to maintain it for as long as he can. That semi-prime is not only red's main offense, his spearhead to safety, it is also his chief defense, since it prevents white from releasing his reserves. Oddly enough, white's position would be much improved if his seven remaining men were on the bar. He would, in fact, become a strong favorite to win the game.

This is another example of the game's paradoxical nature. Two contestants are attempting to mobilize their men around and off the board as speedily as possible, and yet are making moves calculated to slow them down—and both sides are perfectly correct in doing so. But every back game has its built-in potential for self-destruction and it could easily be set off in this position. In this same diagram (#59), suppose white now rolled double 4's. Unable to escape from red's board, he would be forced to tear down his own. Should red then roll a 1 or an 8, white would be sealed in and the remnants of his inner board would be destroyed. Hence, white's position here, though not hopeless, is not auspicious.

Diagram 60 illustrates a back game which has reached the critical point for both factions. Disaster rolls could destroy either position. The worst roll for white is double 3's; for red it is double 5's. This, of course, is the chief drawback to back games; regardless of the painstaking precautions both sides have taken, they are now each in a position where one roll could initiate a landslide. It is that tense moment when both armies, having thrown themselves into the fray, now wait for signs that indicate which side will falter, break and melt away.

At this point, however, white rolls a 5-2. The roll is not as unfortunate as it appears to be. White's mandatory play is to move the 5 from the bar point to the 2 point and the 2 from the 6 point down to the 4 point. Paradoxically, white's main strategy is not to advance his men in his in-

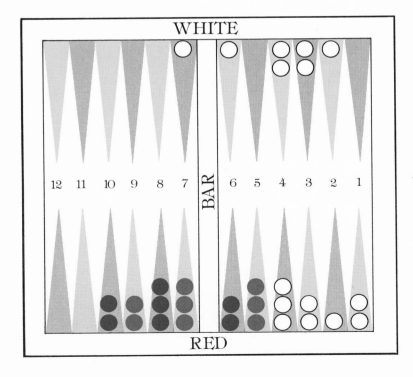

Diagram
60

ner board. He does not want to establish forward positions. And yet to accomplish this, he must move his men down as far as they will go. This tactic saves him from being forced into playing 5's and 6's, gives him breathing space and allows him to delay. At this crucial moment in the game, when victory could turn either way, it would be to each player's advantage to have his opponent roll. They are both employing, or would prefer to employ, delaying tactics.

One strength of white's position is that he has created three points in red's board. On the next roll, should red be forced to break his prime by rolling high numbers, so that his opponent will subsequently have to play from either the 3 or the 4 point, white will still command the 1 point and either the 3 or the 4 point. Assuming that eventually white retained only the 1 and the 3 points, but was forced to break one or the other of them, his position would be tantamount to three soldiers defending their position against an enemy battalion. But with three points secured as they are in the diagram, white's position is not nearly as bad as it looks. As it is, the game is nearly even, although red must be slightly favored because of the threat of the double game. If white had a four-point prime in red's inner board, his first tactic would be to break it so that red would be able to play. In this instance, the open 2 point permits red to play any 6, which otherwise he could not do. It is a delicate situation. The only real reason for white to have four points in red's inner board would be if he had all fifteen of his men distributed on them. White would then be an overwhelming favorite to win. As it stands, however, the tide of the game could turn either way.

In Diagram 61, an illustration of the classic back-game position, white rolls a 2-1. He has three options, the most advantageous of which is to bring one man from red's 1 point to red's 3 point, and to move the outside man from

the 10 to the 11 point. It would be unwise to hit the blot
on red's 2 point, thereby following the general rule for
back games of not hitting, but maintaining a strong defensive position. If white did hit, however, which many players would tend to do, he should then, rather than moving
the outside man, move a man from his own 3 point to his
1 point — giving red 3's, 2's and 1's on which to come in
and hit. In this position, white prefers to be hit. But should
red then roll 4's, 5's or 6's, white's campaign strategy
will have been thwarted and he will probably not be able
to save his board because he is much too far advanced.
Even should red roll his worst possible number, a 1-5, he
would remain in a formidable position. The whole theory
and practice of the back game is illustrated here. However,
if white played correctly — that is, not hitting red's blot on

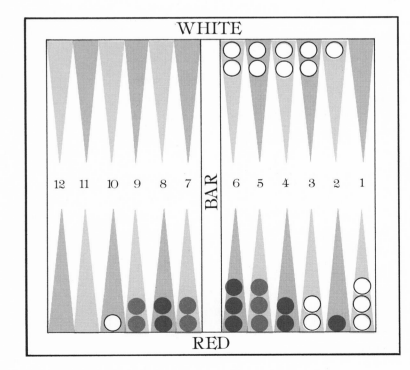

Diagram
61

the 2 point—he is hardly worse than even money to win the game. White's tactic is to force red to play. By hitting, he is sabotaging himself. Incidentally, having four points in his own inner board is a complete illusion of strength at this stage, and white should not place much faith in it for the moment.

There are, however, no moves in backgammon where atrocious plays at certain times cannot become "correct" as a result of subsequent happy rolls. In chess, for example, if white made a foolish play tantamount to hitting red's blot, he would be forced to resign within a few moves. But given the curative powers of the dice in backgammon, the stricken player could well be saved. For instance, suppose that white actually hits red and then moves his outside man up two points. Red then rolls a 1-5, coming in on the 1 point and electing to move a man in, breaking his 9 point. Suppose, further, that white then rolls a 1-6, moving from red's 2 point to hit red's other blot. Red then rolls another 1-5 and is forced to come in on white's 1 point and to move another 5 from his 7 point to his 2 point, as is illustrated in Diagram 62. Red's game has become a disaster, and in light of the results it would be difficult, if not impossible, to convince white (or most fortuitous winners) that he had made the wrong play. Yet such accidents happen all the time.

Most of the basic principles of the back game are illustrated in Diagrams 61, 62 and 63. In Diagram 63, red, having held on to white's 1 and 2 points with six men, managed to time his game perfectly, and after white had borne off twelve men he finally got a shot and hit white's blot on the 3 point. Two rolls later, white rolled a 6-1 to enter red's board and leave it. The position is illustrated at this point. Up to this moment red's back game has been perfectly timed and played, but he still has a long way to go. His problem is not only to catch that lone man of white's

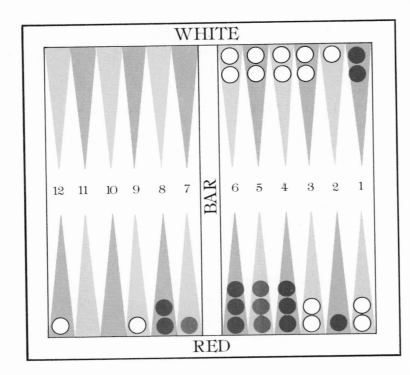

WHITE

12 11 10 9 8 7 **BAR** 6 5 4 3 2 1

RED

Diagram
62

outside, but, if possible, to capture another man, since this is his best chance to win.

Red now rolls a 4-3.

Most players are taught that in situations of the back game's aftermath, they should diversify their men in order to give them a broader base of attack. But unless a block is established somewhere, white's two men on his 4 point are immune to any red assault. The correct play is to move the two men from white's 7 and 8 points up to form a block on white's 11 point. By doing this, red is, in fact, deviously attacking those men. Of course, red could block double 6's, double 5's and double 4's (although double 5's would be to red's advantage, since it would leave two blots; moreover, with double 4's, red is still a favorite to hit). Therefore, by blocking white's 7's, red has made a more practical and far more imaginative play. Now any roll of white's to-

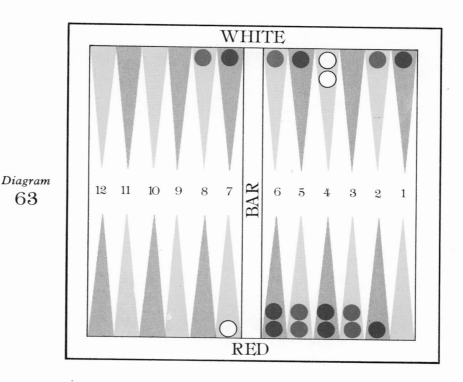

Diagram
63

taling 7 will force him to break the block on his 4 point. It is 5 to 1 against that white will roll a 7, but if he does, red can double and white should drop.

Variations of this situation occur frequently in back games and should be looked for. Again, such plays are entirely a matter of imaginative use of tactical positioning.

It is important to study the intricacies of the back game and not to be cowed by their complications. You must learn to comprehend the reasoning behind such tactics as opening up, hitting and not hitting, blocking and not blocking, and the delicate timing factor; otherwise you will always be at a clever opponent's mercy. Given the entanglements of this type of game, however, and the fact that more often than not it leads to at least a defeat and often a gammon, it cannot be stressed strongly enough that, whenever possible, back games are to be avoided.

◄7►

THE DOUBLER

Capitulation is not a disgrace.
A general can no more entertain the idea
of fighting to the last man than a good
chess player would consider playing an
obviously lost game.
—*Karl von Clausewitz*

The introduction of the doubling block (variously called the *cube* or the *doubler*) is a relatively recent innovation and has added an extraordinary new dimension to the skill of backgammon. The importance of astute use of the doubler is, in fact, difficult to exaggerate. Should an expert player from Armenia, for example, where they do not use the doubler, compete against an average player who is expert in its use (if there is such a phenomenon), the latter would win. The doubler is the key to backgammon.

The doubling block is a large die with numbers ranging from 2 to 4 to 8 to 16 to 32 to 64. At the beginning of any game, this die rests at the side of the board and is brought into play by whichever player thinks he has the first advantage. Either player may double or redouble only when it is his turn to roll, and only *before* he rolls. For example, if one player believes he is ahead at any moment in a game being played at 10¢/$1/$10 or whatever a point, he may double his opponent to 2. (Without the doubler, one point is scored for winning a single game.) Either player may make the first double, but having done so, he may not double again until redoubled by his opponent. If the opponent wishes, he retires, or declines the double, thereby losing 1 point—or 10¢, $1 or $10. If he accepts, however, the stakes are now at 2, or 20¢, $2 or $20, and should he find himself ahead at a later stage in the game, he may double back to 4, thus increasing the worth of the game to 40¢, $4 or $40 if his opponent accepts it. (Incidentally, just because the last number on the die is 64 does not mean the doubling stops there. Theoretically, the degree of doubling is unlimited and can go on to 128, 256 512, and so on, though in an expert game the doubler rarely rises above 4. The reason for this is the respect expert players have for the doubler.)

Further, occasionally at the beginning of a game, both players, rolling one die, may roll the same number. By prior arrangement, the doubler may then begin at 2. These are called automatic doubles, but they play no part in the strategy of backgammon, nor are they ever used in tournaments. They are only employed in certain money games as a means of increasing the stakes.

A volume could be written on the doubler alone. Assume, as so often happens, that someone shows you a certain backgammon position and then asks: "Should red double and should white accept?" Given this scant information, the question is meaningless. In order to answer the question accurately, one must also know who is playing whom. Is it a tournament match, and if so, what is the score? What are the relative skills of the opponents? Is it a money game? Is red redoubling or is this the first double? How high are the stakes? Is it a chouette, and if so, how many players are involved? These are just a few of the factors that must be clarified in order to answer the question.

The longer one considers the doubler, the more complex it seems to become. Does your opponent tend to take doubles? If so, wait until his position is nearly hopeless. Is he prone to dropping early? Then offer him a double against the odds in the hope that he will. Here, as in other areas of backgammon, adapting your game to your adversary's is vital. The taking of a double against player A would be a certain drop against player B. You should double player C early and be more cautious against player D. More often than not, the unobservant player merely examines the position on the board. For instance, if white doubles red in the situation in Diagram 64, red with a block on white's 5 point, and white with several men still to transport into his inner board, red should accept if white is the stronger player, whereas he should

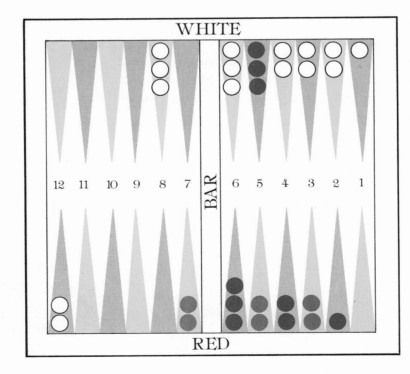

Diagram
64

drop if red is an expert pitted against a weaker player, since there is little expertise left in this game. The doubler is a razor-sharp boomerang and it could be suicidal to allow it to fall into the wrong hands. Therefore, the giving of a double depends not only on the position of the moment but on the psychological make-up and technical ability of your adversary.

To comprehend the theory inherent in the doubler is probably the most important part of backgammon. The thrifty use of this instrument can launch an ordinary player into the higher echelons of the game. Beginners are invariably taught not to take "bad doubles." Of course the advice is sound and sensible, but there is a corollary which is even more sensible: Do not drop when you should take. *Unquestionably, the greatest number of points lost in backgammon is by players refusing doubles they should have taken.* One should not take bad doubles, but a more positive philosophy is: When in doubt, take. Consider the fact that if you take four doubles and lose three of them, you are still even—presupposing, of course, that no gammons are involved. This phenomenon will be examined later in the chapter; for the moment, accustom yourself to accepting playable doubles. Few players understand the leverage they acquire by taking a double. By doing so and by not redoubling until the right moment, you are in the game to the end. Even if the roof falls in, you can still take advantage of every miracle roll to extricate yourself.

Generally speaking, then, when do you take a double? If you are less than a 3 to 1 underdog and there is no danger of losing a double game, you should take a double every time in money games. It may seem odd to allow the stakes to be doubled when you are an underdog, but consider the logic of the matter. Assume the stake is $1 a point and you are doubled by your opponent. If you drop, you lose $1. If you take the double, you risk losing one additional dollar—that is, $2. On the other hand, if you win the game, you *win* $2. Thus, your net position, instead of being −1 (if you had refused the double) is now +2, a difference of 3. So by taking a double and winning, you are $3 better off than you would have been if you had dropped. You have won $3 while only risking one additional dollar. Therefore, any time you are less than a 3 to 1 underdog, you should accept a double.

In Diagram 65, white has two men on his 2 point and red has two men on his 1 point. All their other men have been borne off. At this point, white doubles. Should red accept? In money games, the answer is yes, yet time after

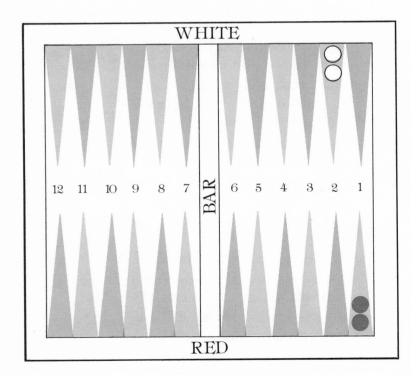

Diagram
65

time people drop in this position. Sometimes a player will say, "I'd take if I were being doubled from 2 to 4, but not when it's from 32 to 64." This kind of specious reasoning is cowardly and exasperating. If it is a take from 2 to 4, it is just as much a take from 32 to 64. How many combinations does white require to bear off both men on this roll? The answer is 26. All 1's except double 1's prevent him from coming off—a total of 10 unfavorable combinations. Thus, the odds are 26 to 10, or 13 to 5, in favor of white. The fraction 13 to 5 is less than 3 to 1, and since red is getting 3 to 1 for his additional dollar, he should accept. This is a basic rule of thumb for accepting doubles. On the other hand, white is perfectly correct in doubling, since he is a 13 to 5 favorite to win. Here is an example where one player doubles, his opponent takes, and both are correct.

Obviously, to want to double the stakes, you have to be ahead, but it is a matter of opinion just how *far* you should be ahead. In our opinion, if it is possible to compute, you should be at least a 3 to 2 favorite when you offer the first double, but you should be a minimum favorite of 2 to 1 to redouble. The reason for this discrepancy is that before the first double is offered, the cube is in the public domain; that is, either player has access to it and may employ it. But once you have been doubled, the cube becomes your property and can never be taken away from you. It is the most potent weapon in your arsenal and you should be wary of releasing it. You should wait, in fact, until you are fairly certain that your adversary will capitulate.

There are occasions when your position becomes overwhelmingly powerful within a few moves and the opportunity for a gammon arises. In this case, do not double—unless your opponent has a point in your inner board, in which case you should double him out.

In other words, avoid playing for a gammon (usually

in tournaments and almost always in money games) if your opponent has a block on your 1 point and a potential board—that is, when he has no men out of play. This holds true regardless of how many of his men you have on the bar. You are in jeopardy until the game is over, not to mention the jolting psychological blow of losing a hard-fought game at the eleventh hour. The enemy is too apt to get one or more shots before the game ends. Here the risk rarely justifies the rewards.

One of the persistent curiosities of the doubler is that if you refuse a double in three consecutive games and are right twice and wrong once, you are losing money. This is proved again and again in chouettes, where one player is pitted against two or more players, and where it is often possible to witness the outcome of a game after you have dropped. Consider (assuming, of course, no gammons): if you drop three times, you are −3. If you had taken all three doubles, you would be −2, −2 and +2, for a net of −2, or 1 point better off than those who dropped all three games.* But it is difficult to convince someone who has just been right two out of three times that he is wrong. Wrong he is, however, and the sooner he understands it, the wealthier— or less poor—he will be.

A few general random rules

If you have accepted a double, and, later on in the game get a direct shot (25 to 11 against) which, if you hit, will win the game for you, the acceptance of the double has been vindicated. (Again, this presupposes no gammons.) In the long run, your take will have been justified

---

*There is an interesting psychological factor at work here, which will be discussed in Chapter Eleven.

even if in this specific instance you do not hit the blot. This is just another way of saying that you were less than a 3 to 1 underdog, since 25 to 11 is approximately 2¼ to 1.

Let us assume that you have borne off several of your men, but in doing so leave a triple shot. If your opponent misses, he is in great danger of losing a double game, but he doubles anyway. Most players look at the triple shot as though they had seen a ghost; they blanch and drop. But they should take. The odds are 3 to 1 in your opponent's favor, which you will remember is the dividing line for taking doubles; therefore the take per se is even money. But you have an excellent chance for a double game if your opponent misses, and so what you stand to gain by taking makes it, in effect, a winning proposition financially.

Regarding "late" doubles: A moot position often arises in a chouette (discussed in detail in the next chapter) when some members of the partnership wish to double the box and others do not. Assume the final decision to be not to double. The captain then rolls a perfect roll, destroying his opponent's position. Those who had advocated doubling now complain that it was wrong not to have doubled before, when the box would have accepted. On the next roll the captain doubles, the box drops, and recriminations multiply.

Two important factors are generally overlooked in these situations. The captain could not have known that he was about to roll the perfect shot; in fact, the odds were against it. More importantly, by waiting one roll, the partners now have the money in their pockets, whereas if they had doubled earlier and it had been accepted, the box would still be in the game with a chance to win. Any time you can force your opponent to drop, you have accomplished a great deal. More than anything else, the dice are to be respected, for they have all the power. By doubling and making your opponent surrender, instead of merely raising the stakes, you show your respect for the dice and sever their hold on the outcome of the game.

If the doubler is on your side and you roll a shot which turns the game around so that you will be able to redouble on the next roll, you must be sure to take no impetuous risks with any part of that roll. Do not give your opponent an opportunity to roll the perfect retaliatory shot. In Diagram 66, white has a 5-1 to play. Given the fact that the doubler is on white's side, the correct play here is to move from red's 3 point to his 8 point, hitting his blot, and to move the man from white's bar point to his 6 point. This play thwarts the potential miracle rolls of 1-6 and 5-2 by red. For regardless of whether or not red comes in,

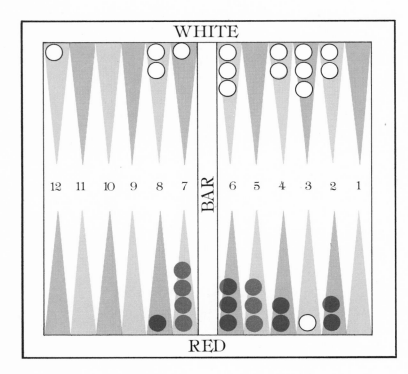

Diagram 66

white is ready to redouble on almost all return rolls by red, and does not need to take any risks. To save the 1 is not cowardly; it is using the doubler to win the game. You would make this play if the doubler was in the middle or on your side. On the other hand, if the doubler is in red's corner, white should make his best tactical play—that is, to hit red's blot and to use the 1 to make his bar point, thereby giving red only a 5-3 to hit. Because white cannot use the doubler to knock red from the game, the duel will be won or lost on the field; hence, white must make his best tactical maneuver. Here again it can be seen how the doubler influences the action, circumscribes one's choices and dictates the way in which the men are moved.

In Diagram 67, red has been doubled and owns the

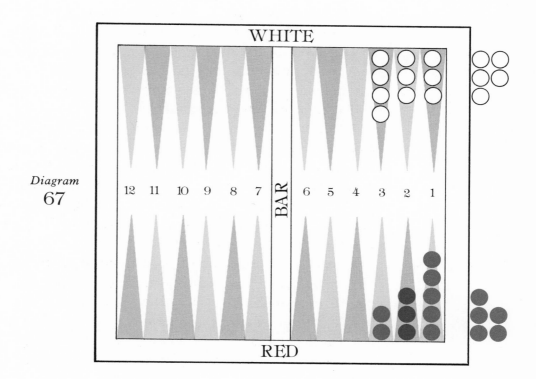

Diagram 67

cube. The game develops into a race, and both players reach a position where they have five men off and the other ten distributed more or less equally on their 1, 2 and 3 points. But it is red's roll. Does red redouble? Not yet. It is true that red is ahead in a race, and if no doubles are thrown, he will win. But if red releases the doubler now and white rolls a double and red does not, white can redouble and red will have to drop.

A sound rule to follow about redoubling when bearing off: If both players have five rolls left (that is, ten men positioned on the lower points), wait. You may consider redoubling with four rolls left, depending on your opponent, and you must *always* redouble with three. If both players are left with six men—which is three more rolls—and you redouble now, your opponent has no equity in owning the cube. Let us say you roll and take two men off. Now he rolls a double, taking four men off. You still have a chance to roll a double and win, and since it is not his turn, he cannot double you out of the game beforehand. Thus, when each combatant has six men remaining on the lower points, the redouble is mandatory.

If neither side has doubled and the cube is in the middle, you may offer a double much earlier, since you are giving up no equity. If you can calculate that there are seven rolls apiece remaining, offer the first double immediately. The redouble, however, is another proposition; in that case you are trying to double your opponent out of the game, not to double the stakes.

In advocating "takes" as a general winning philosophy, we should issue one warning. Beware of the completely emotional take to which many players are vulnerable. In chouettes, for example, over the years we have seen dozens of players join the game late. The box will offer an early double and the new player will examine the position, then drop, though he is no more than a 7 to 5 underdog in the game. The chouette continues and the new player hits a bad streak and falls behind. At this point he gets into the box, becomes involved in a hopeless position and is open to losing a double game. He is now offered a double by his opponents and accepts.

This kind of neurotic take is suicidal, deserves to be punished, and usually is. When deciding whether or not to take a double, remember to analyze each position, each acceptance or refusal, on its merits alone. Ignore the score in a money game and try to estimate whether or not you are a 3 to 1 underdog or less, with no double-game dangers. If this is the case, accept the double; if it is not, regardless of how you feel or how lucky you believe your opponent to have been, drop and get on with the next game.

To sum up: When in doubt, take; when in doubt, do *not* double. In backgammon, it is better to be a taker than a giver.

Though not included in the official laws of backgammon, there is another wrinkle to the use of the doubler, in which one contestant may *beaver* his opponent—provided both parties have agreed beforehand to allow beavers. In this further refinement the player who has been doubled not only has the right to accept, but immediately, *before* his opponent rolls, may redouble and *retain* the cube. Thus, if player A doubles player B to 2, B can accept and redouble to 4 before A rolls, yet still retain the right to redouble to 8 whenever he wishes.

This addition is colorful and escalates the gambling ingredient, but in an expert game you will hardly ever see a beaver being offered. By itself the single take will be enough, because the expert knows what he's doing and will not offer a rash double.

The Use of the Doubler in Tournaments

When you sit down against any opponent, always hesitate when he offers you the first double—unless it's a clear take, in which case you should accept so gleefully that it may make him unsure of himself. But if you're going to drop, don't hurry. Look over the board, regardless of the position, and appear to consider taking the double. In bridge such a ploy would be unethical, but in backgammon and poker this tactic is completely acceptable. Doing this creates the impression that you hate to drop (which, on principle, you should), and so your opponent will tend to be more cautious in the future about increasing the stake. As a result, you may get a free ride for several rolls later on, during which you may throw the miracle roll that turns the game around.

Whatever else may be said of it, the doubler is a particularly lethal weapon in tournament play, where it can actually favor the weaker player—if only he recognized its power and knew when and where to exert it. Not long ago, for example, a comparative beginner drew an expert in the opening round of an important tournament. It was a 15-point match, the score was 6–3 in favor of the expert. In the next game the expert gave the beginner an early double, almost expecting him to drop because *he* had doubled. But the beginner was not so easily cowed; he accepted and the doubler was now at 2 on his side. The game continued, swinging back and forth, and several moves later, one of the beginner's men was captured and placed on the bar. The expert, white, had a five-point board, but had a blot on his 4 point, as well as two additional blots in his outer board. The beginner had managed to construct a prime, as is illustrated in Diagram 68.

As the beginner (red) prepared to roll, he was more

than a 2 to 1 underdog (25 to 11, to be exact) to come in on white's 4 point. But had the beginner thought of it, there was a clever doubling tactic to be employed in this position. Even though he is the underdog, it is imperative that he now redouble. In order to overcome the expert, he will have to win this game; thus he must double against the odds. In this position the expert would prefer not to be doubled. If the beginner rolls a 4, he will deal the expert a stunning psychological blow; he will almost certainly win 8 points, and the match will be in jeopardy.

This is just one example of how a beginner can use the doubler to compensate for his opponent's superior technical abilities. If the beginner fails to hit the blot, he will fall behind 10–3 or possibly even 14–3. But if he hits,

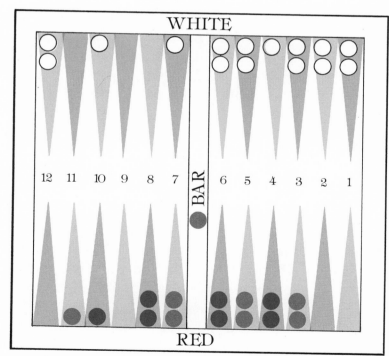

Diagram
68

the score could be 11–6 in his favor. It is an immense opportunity and should be taken; in the parlance of baseball, it is not a time to bunt, but to hit away. (Needless to add, were the positions reversed, an expert would be most inexpert were he to redouble here.)

Whether or not the tyro hit the blot is irrelevant. The point is that like so many others in similar positions, he failed to recognize his opportunities. The thought of redoubling never crossed his mind.

Situations of this kind occur repeatedly in tournaments, and the inexperienced player tends to be too timid or too naïve to capitalize on the leverage he has in the doubler. Of course the doubler is a two-edged threat, but the beginner can make use of it in a way no expert would consider doing. He must learn to recognize and then to snatch these major opportunities.

Tournament tactics differ in many ways from money games and chouette. In tournaments, the only objective is to defeat your adversary, and the difference in your scores is immaterial; to win 15–0 or 15–14 is the same. Those 14 points have cost you nothing, whereas in a money game, you would be charged 14 times the stake. Let us assume that you have an 11–1 lead in a 15-point tournament match. Early in the next game, your opponent has a remote chance, should everything go right for him, of winning a gammon. In the tournament you would drop if he doubles, remaining ahead 11–2; in money games, you would take every time. The strategies of the two types of play are vastly different. Indeed, the tactics are so dissimilar that it is as though you were playing with a different set of rules. This vital factor should have an enormous effect on how you handle the doubler during your different matches. At different times in the same match in a tournament, it is possible to arrive at two identical positions which, in the one case, you would drop if doubled, and in the other you would take.

A familiarity with the numerous complexities of the Crawford Rule is essential, and it is surprising that so few players trouble themselves with this crucial adjunct to tournament play.

The Crawford Rule stipulates that in, for example, a 15-point match, when one player reaches 14 and his opponent has a lesser score, the player who is behind may not double in the first subsequent game. When that game has been completed, however, he may then double at will. This rule applies each time one player is a point from victory; it is used in American tournaments, but not as yet abroad. The Crawford Rule is an attempt to protect the player with the greater score, but in our view it does not go far enough. A fairer rule would be one that prohibits your opponent from winning more points than you can potentially win in any one game. For example, in a 15-point match, if player A is ahead 1–0, the most player B could win in the next game would be 14. If player B is ahead 10–7, the most player A could win would be 5, and so on.

The difference in tactics when the Crawford Rule is in use is complicated and far-reaching. Suppose that you are playing an opponent just as skillful as you are, and the score is 13–13 in a 15-point match. What will your doubling strategy be in this crucial game? Should you double early, late or neither when the Crawford Rule is in effect? The answer is that you should tend to double earlier than usual, because you give up no leverage; that is, he has no advantage in owning the cube, since if he accepts, it will be the last game and there is no point in redoubling. Secondly, he is almost forced to take the double, since if he drops, he must win the next two games (barring gammons) to win the match. Therefore, by doubling you have reduced this match to a one-game proposition, in which you have a slight edge—obviously correct tactics.

The only time you should not double in this situation is if there is an inkling of a double game. In this case, you must go for it—of course taking every precaution not to lose a double game yourself. This latter strategy applies whether the Crawford Rule is in effect or not.

But in the exact same situation—that is, a 15-point match which is drawn 13–13, and no Crawford Rule— your doubling tactics are altogether different. There is no redouble here either, but in this instance your opponent has nothing to gain by accepting the double. Therefore he would drop and double you at the beginning of the next game. Your best tactic in this situation is to go all out to win a double game and the match—again attempting to en- sure that you do not lose a double game yourself. Your first priority, then, is to set up a defense to prevent that possi- bility. Having accomplished this, you must try to secure the gammon, even at the risk of losing a single game.

In this situation, at what point *should* you double? The answer, regardless of the strength or weakness of your position, is "almost never." If you double and he drops, you have won nothing, for the 1 point you have won is useless. Being ahead 14–13 only gives you the dubious privilege of dropping on the next game after the opening roll, when your opponent will certainly double you.

There is one specific exception to this rule. As is evi- dent in Diagram 69, red is vulnerable to losing a gammon and the match if he does not hit one of white's two blots. He has been in danger of losing a double game throughout, but now he unexpectedly finds himself a 5 to 4 favorite to win the match if he doubles. Since red will in all probability lose a gammon if he misses, he has nothing to lose here by doubling. He might just as well lose 4 as 2, since either

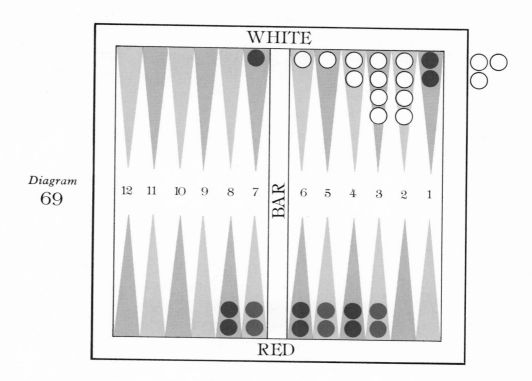

Diagram 69

loss will cost him the match. This is the kind of situation in which the thoughtless player will not consider a double, since he is so relieved at the possibility of saving a double game, but this is specious reasoning. Failing to double at this critical juncture is a deplorable blunder; it is tantamount to losing by default. This is his opportunity to win at no extra risk to himself; therefore red must double.

White's tactics in this game have been absolutely correct. He has been going all out to win a double game, and since he has three men off, he now cannot lose a double game. Therefore he is able to play as recklessly as he chooses — unless red thwarts his plans by doubling, thereby putting him in danger of losing the match, from which he has hitherto been exempt. It is a marvelous moment for the bold and unexpected counterattack.

Given red's crushing double, should white take or not? It depends entirely on the respective abilities of the players. If white is clearly the better player, he should drop, since in this special situation he is a 5 to 4 underdog. If he drops, the score will be 14–13 against him, but he will have a better than even chance in the next game. Why should white allow himself to become an underdog when he is the favorite? But if white is much the weaker player, he should take, since at the moment he is only a 5 to 4 underdog, whereas if he dropped, he would be much more of an underdog in the next game, given the superiority of his opponent.

Incidentally, in all money games, if red doubles in this position, white should take every time. He is only a 5 to 4 underdog, which is less than 3 to 1, in addition to which he has excellent gammon expectations. You may recall the question at the beginning of this chapter about whether or not to take a double in a certain position. This is a perfect example of that decision being dependent on many different factors. In one case, you take; in the other, you drop— and in both cases, the position is exactly the same. This is just one more indication of the kind of fluid reasoning backgammon requires.

The kind of reasoning and logic involved in the previous example will, if heeded, improve your game in all departments. It is worth remembering, since even experts are wont to overlook the subtleties of the doubler. In a recent tournament, two of the world's top players, tied at 9–9 in an 11-point match, reached the position in Diagram 70. In this position, red doubled and white took. Not only was it an atrocious take, it was an even more atrocious double. It is difficult to determine which player exhibited the greater folly. This is another example of translating your prerogatives from one context to another. In a money

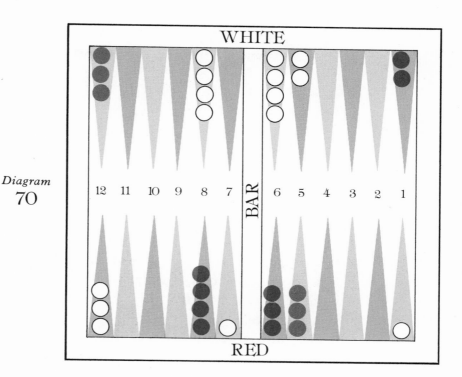

Diagram
70

game, this is a definite take, but in a tournament with this score and no Crawford Rule, the position must be seen in a different light, since different tactics now apply.

If white drops, he has lost 1 point, which means next to nothing. True, he has given his opponent a free drop (see next page) on the next game after the opening roll, but this is a minuscule edge compared with the benefits he gains from dropping here. Since in the next game he will double at once and put the match on the line, to take the double in this dodgy position is absurd. And what does red gain by doubling? He assumes that white is going to drop, and so anticipates gaining one point. What red should have done in this position was to go for the double game.

What actually happened was that white took the double and won the game and the match. Red was furious that white's ineptitude had been rewarded. White, having won, defended his take, insisting that *his* was the correct play.

White was challenged by a third party for a sizable wager; he could, said the third party, pick five independent experts, and if any *one* of them agreed with white's decision, he would win the wager. After much waffling, white backed down. This is yet another example of how a player's ego can obstruct his reason, causing him to justify an arrogant and indefensible play.

We mentioned a tactic called the *free drop*. When you have reached 14 in a 15-point match and your opponent has some lesser *odd* number—such as 5—you may utilize what is known as a free drop. If your opponent opens with, say, a roll of 3-1 and you now roll a 5-2, you should drop if he doubles. There is no logical reason to play out the game in this position when you must play with even the smallest of handicaps. Dropping does not significantly affect the score, and given the respective opening rolls, your position is now inferior to his. The reason why the score is not particularly affected is that your opponent still requires the same number of victories to win the match. At 14–5, and assuming he doubles on the first roll of every game, since he loses nothing by doing so, he requires five victories in order to reach 15 and to win. At 14–6, he *still* requires five victories to reach 15. You must learn to use this free drop at your first opportunity. Most players know enough to do this when the score is 14–13, but you can apply the same principle to any odd number. However, the number must be odd; it would be madness to let your opponent run from even to odd. Thus, dropping in situations of this kind is an excellent tactic to employ.

Tournament play is replete with sly conundrums that

do not exist in money games. Hence, tournament play demands not only different skills, but more exacting ones. For example, when you reach 14 in a 15-point match with the Crawford Rule in effect, it is always preferable to have your opponent at some lesser odd number. You *prefer* him to be odd. Conversely, if the final goal is an even number, you want him at an even number. But the reverse is true when the Crawford Rule is not in effect. Whether your opponent's score is odd or even will not alter your strategy to any great degree, but it is worth knowing whether you want your opponent at an odd or even number. It can influence your accepting a double, for example.

Regardless of whether or not the Crawford Rule is in use, when you get within 2 points of your goal, say 13 in a 15-point match, try your utmost to win a double game. To be within 1 point of your goal makes you vulnerable as soon as all restrictions on the doubler are released. It is not an enviable position, since in every game you play for the rest of the match, you can lose, given backgammons, as many as 6 points, whereas the most you can win is 1. Therefore it is best to attempt to hurdle over 14 from 13 by attempting to win the double game. Furthermore, if you are at 13 and your opponent is at some lesser number, tend to take doubles if you are in doubt, because if you win the game you win the match.

Again, this is a paradox. To be at 14 is naturally better than being at 13. Even so, at 14 you have problems which would not otherwise exist. Your opponent controls the doubler, and it is of little or no benefit to you. He may double immediately at the beginning of every game *at no risk*. It is true that he might also double immediately if you were at 13, but he does so here at great risk, since you can win not only the game but the match, which would not have been true had he not doubled.

These details regarding unique or special uses of the doubler are vital educational aids for the ambitious player, and they are not difficult to learn or to remember.

Losing a gammon is the bugaboo of all backgammon players; it is the prevailing danger against which players are warned from the very beginning. Yet in tournaments there are situations where the loss of a double game is virtually no worse than losing a single game. Though most players fail to grasp this concept, it is a great advantage for those who do. But it only occurs in special situations.

In a 15-point match, the score is 14–12 (or any lesser even number) in favor of white, in Diagram 71. White has a man on the bar and now rolls a 4-1. Ordinarily you are taught to try to save a double game, but in this instance it

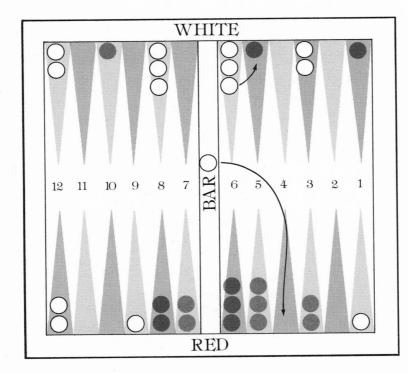

Diagram 71

is irrelevant, since you have virtually nothing to lose. If your opponent gets to 14–14 in this particular game, he is not much better off than if he were at 14–13 with his doubling privilege restored. The small advantage of the free drop is forfeited by white if he decides to go for the win and thereby loses a gammon, but it is worth it to attempt to clinch the match on this game. The main danger to watch for is the loss of a triple game. In this position, were white to come in on the 1 point and play the 4 elsewhere, he might even save a double game. But these should not be his tactics. If he comes in on the 4 point, hits red's blot on his 5 point and gets away with this bold play, it is his best chance to win the game and the match even though he is a distinct underdog to do so. However, it is most important that he avoid losing a triple game, but oddly enough, by coming in on the 4 point instead of the 1, he has minimized this danger. Triple games usually occur when a player holds his adversary's 1 point and remains there for a long time. In sum, our recommended move is a bold but necessary play.

A variation of this principle occurred in another tournament match. The match was being played to 15 and the score was 14–8 in favor of red. In the position shown in Diagram 72, white, having waited intentionally, now doubled. In both tournaments and money games, red would tend to drop, but given the score—that is, 14 to any lesser *even* number—red should take every time.

The subtle logic here is that since white is at 8, he needs four consecutive victories to win the match—excluding double games and assuming that it is legal for him to double and that he does so in each successive game after the opening roll. But if he were at 9 instead of at 8, he would need only three victories to win the match. Therefore, since being at 9 is virtually as good as being at 10, white should double, hoping to bluff red into dropping. In over 90 percent of such cases the bluff would work. If white accomplishes this, he has, in effect, won a game by default and increased his chances of winning the match because he now needs only three victories instead of four.

On the other hand, in this instance red should take the double, regardless of the hopelessness of his position—unless, of course, there were any danger of losing a gammon. Should red accept the double and lose, the score will now be 14–10 in his favor, which is barely worse than 14–9. The point being that the man who is behind is always trying to get from even to odd, and this is what red is trying to obstruct. Since the comparative values of 9 and 10 are almost the same, red accepts what appears to be an insane double (which in all money games he would drop)

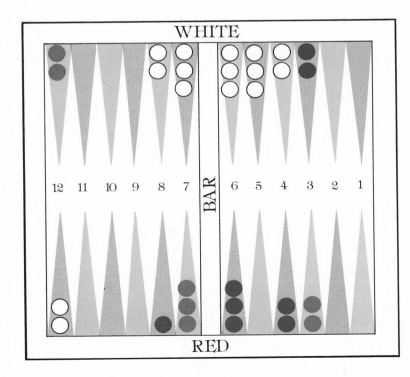

WHITE

12 11 10 9 8 7 BAR 6 5 4 3 2 1

RED

Diagram
72

because if he loses this game he has lost nothing extra, and if he should win, he wins the match.

Any time you have a substantial lead on the score in a tournament and have accepted a double, there is almost no position which will arise subsequently in which you should redouble. For example, in a recent tournament an expert was playing an average player in a 23-point match. Red was ahead 18–11 (certainly a substantial lead) and had accepted a double to 2 from white, the expert. The position then changed in red's favor and he redoubled to 4. White accepted, and a roll or two later, though still well behind, he redoubled to 8. The reason for the redouble is obvious. If white loses at 4, he will be behind even more, 22–11, and is virtually out of the match. Therefore this is a must game for him—hence the redouble. As luck would have it, disaster struck red and white won a gammon or 16 points, winning the match 27–18. Red had no one to blame but himself. He broke a cardinal rule by redoubling in the first place and deserved precisely what he got. If you redouble in such circumstances, you are giving your opponent enormous leverage and have reserved none for yourself. Had red won the game at 2, he would have held a 20–11 lead; even had he lost the 2, he would still have led 18–13. Thus, red in effect threw the game away.

In tournament play, *one* game can determine the outcome of the match. This is more true of tournaments than of money games or chouettes. The game is a series of all-or-nothing skirmishes, and unlike war, all victories are complete and absolute. The point to remember is that nothing in backgammon is irrelevant. There are no flights of fancy, no odds and ends. Everything is built upon something else—logic upon logic upon logic. And at the heart of it all is the doubler—the ruling element without which backgammon would be just another lottery. Unless the beginner understands the doubler, he, like the gentleman from Armenia, will never be more than an average competitor.

The Pip Count

The so-called pip count is an inexact method of determining which side is ahead, and by how much, after all contact between the sides has ceased—that is, when both armies have maneuvered their forces beyond one another and there will be no further contact by either side.

To determine your own and your opponent's pip count is simple but tedious arithmetic. Any men on your 1 point count 1 point apiece, the men on your 2 point count 2 points apiece and so on throughout the board. There are a total of 24 points, so should you have any men on your opponent's 1 point, they would count 24 apiece. Obviously there would still be contact were this the case, however, and logically speaking the pip count would not be employed in this instance.

At the beginning of the game, each player has a count of 167. When you understand how this figure is determined, you will be able to make an accurate count of both your position and your opponent's at any stage during the game. Your two men in your opponent's inner board are 24 apiece, or 48. Your five men on his 12 point are 13 apiece, or 65. The three men on your 8 point are 8 apiece, or 24, and the five men on your 6 point are 6 apiece, or 30—making a total of 167.

Should you be considering doubling, the following formula is normally applied to ascertain the relative positions of both sides. If the pip count for both sides is over 100, you should be between 15 and 20 pips ahead to double, but at least 20 ahead to redouble. (Remember that the lower your pip count is, the farther you are ahead.) Conversely, tend to take a double if you are less than 20 pips behind and perhaps drop if over 20. We say "perhaps," since we naturally dislike dropping in these positions. There is no chance of a double game, and the game still has a long way to go. If both sides are between 90 and 100 pips, you should be at least 13 pips ahead to double; between 80 and 90, 10 pips ahead; between 70 and 80, 7; and between 60 and 70, 5.

When both sides are under 50 pips, the basic fallacies in the pip count begin to become evident. We do not recommend using the pip count at all, but particularly when the count is under 50. The amount of time and effort it takes to add this, that and these; to make the same computations for your opponent; and then to subtract one from the other in order to decide whether or not to double, addles the brain and depletes energy that could be put to better use determining tactics and strategies in the ensuing game. Make no mistake, when you begin to take backgammon seriously, stamina—both mental and physical—becomes a salient requirement, and the pip count is a particularly exhausting and essentially useless form of mental calisthenics. In baseball terms, it is a bit like requiring the pitcher to warm up between innings. As it is, the astute backgammon player is making enough continuous calculations without resorting to additional arithmetic.

The basic fallacy of the pip count can be shown in many ways. Consider the position shown in Diagram 73. White has two men on the 1 point, two on the 2 point and two on the 3 point, for a pip count of 12. Red has two men on the 3 point and four men on the 1 point, a pip count of 10. If it is white's roll, there can be no argument that red should refuse the double. But if it were red's roll—

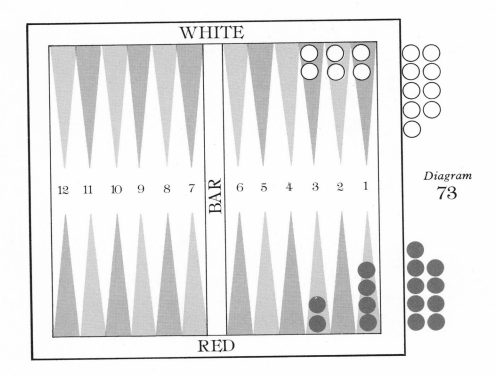

Diagram **73**

remember that he is 2 pips ahead—and he doubled, white would have a clear-cut take. If red rolled any 2 except double 2's, white should even redouble. In other words, with only three rolls or less remaining in the game, white, who is *behind* in the pip count doubles and his opponent must drop. And in the same position, if the pip-count leader doubled, his opponent would have to take. This example also shows that when bearing off the even diversification of your men in your inner board is infinitely more important than the pip count.

In Diagram 74, red has two men left on his 6 point, a pip count of 12, and white has three men on his 1 point, a pip count of 3. Red is 9 pips behind, it is his roll and he has a mandatory double. So much for the pip count.

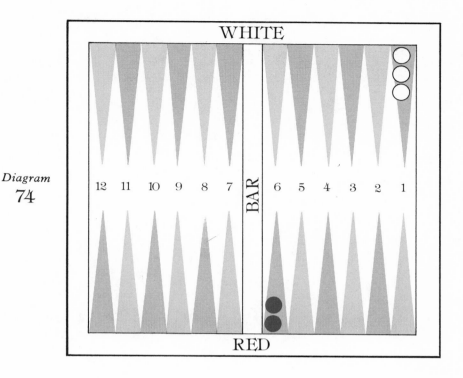

Diagram 74

If you have been playing backgammon for a long period, you should be able to determine your position and your opponent's at a glance and know whether or not you are less than 3 to 1 to win. Even so, there are players who continue to use the pip count despite the fact that it is little more than a long detour toward the same goal; it is reminiscent of the awkward counting movements beginners employ when moving their men about the board. Use it if you must, if it actually helps you, but if you learn to recognize the game's position at any given moment in the match, you will have accomplished a great deal more and in far less time.

◄8►

CHOUETTE

War is a constant state of reciprocal
action, the effects of which are mutual.

— *Karl von Clausewitz*

The three principal methods of playing backgammon are head-to-head, tournaments and chouette — that is, one person playing against a field of two or more players. Because it is not a duel, chouette in its broadest sense is the most civilized and social form of the game, inspiring both competitiveness and camaraderie.

Chouette is organized in an order of strict rotation. Any number of players may participate, but an ideal group is four or five. To begin a chouette, each player rolls a single die. The one who rolls the highest number is called *the man in the box* or simply *the box,* and he competes against all the others. The man rolling the second highest number becomes *the captain* of the opposing side, and he will play and roll the dice. All others become the captain's partners, and though for the moment they cannot play, they may confer with the captain on all his moves and act as a kind of general staff. But though they may advise, they are ultimately bound by all the captain's decisions, except when offered a double; then, regardless of what the captain does, they may accept or refuse as they see fit.

Throughout play, the rotation order is maintained. If the man in the box wins, he remains there, the defeated captain goes to the bottom of the order and each player in turn becomes the new captain. If, however, the captain wins, he becomes the new holder of the box, displacing the man who has just lost, and who is now relegated to the bottom of the order on the opposing team.

In the scoring of chouette, the box competes against each of the other players. If he is playing against, say, four opponents and wins a 1-point game, he is +4 and each of the others is −1. On the other hand, if the box loses, he is −4 and each of the other players is +1.

During a game the box may double and the captain may decide to retire, but one or more of his advisers may decide to accept the double. If this occurs, the player closest to the top of the rotation who has accepted becomes the captain and plays. If he wins, he becomes the man in the box and the other players rotate in the normal way. A partner who decides not to accept a double is no longer in the game and cannot advise the captain further, but by declining a double, he does not lose his place in the order of play.

Because the man in the box is alone, it has been claimed that there is a small but definite percentage operating against him. The reason put forward for this is that if he makes a miscalculation, it will not be pointed out to him, whereas if the captain of the opposing side blunders, he has two, three or even more advisers who can spot and correct their captain's error before he picks up his dice. It is assumed that because there are four minds at work on the same problem, there is less margin for error, and that therefore the percentages are in their favor. This is probably true, but the box has compensating advantages. Because he is playing by himself, he can make the moves of his choice without interference or argument and need neither explain nor defend his tactics to anyone. More importantly, he is given the privilege of preempting any and all deals among the other players. Concerning deals and settlements, he is the game's sole judge and adjudicator.

For instance, a controversy may arise as to whether or not to double the box. Let us assume that the captain—player A—and player B wish to double, but that C and D think it a poor idea. Further, let us assume that those preferring to double offer to buy out the objectors by giving them a point apiece for their respective games. An agreement is reached and the captain now doubles. The man in the box now has various options. He may agree to play all four games or to drop them. Or he may preempt either or both of C and D's games; that is, according to the laws of chouette, he can give C 1 point and play three games, or he can give both C and D a point apiece and play the other two games. This rule is an enormous advantage to him, since it gives him a greater scope should he wish to hedge.

On the other hand, assume that the box doubles everybody. Each contestant decides whether or not he will accept the double. Player A decides to refuse; player B, on the other hand, decides it is a clear-cut take and not only takes it himself, but offers to take player A's game as well. Again the man in the box has the right to veto the arrangement, insisting that player A drop to him and not to one of the other players.

Whenever any settlement is made among the other players, the box gets first acceptance or refusal, regardless of the amount. He has all claims of prior right. Suppose the bearing-off stage has been reached and a blot has been left. This is a settlement situation (the intricacies of which we will discuss in the next chapter). All kinds of demands and offers are heard—not only among the partnership, but between the box and the partnership. Again, if any agreements are reached between the other players, the box has the right to intervene and take the settlement for himself.

Thus, on balance, despite the fact that the box is alone, we believe that the percentages are in his favor rather than against him. The vital point to remember in chouette is that the important games are those played in the box. Whenever you are in the box, therefore, remember that these are the decisive battles and that the degree of your gains and losses will be settled here.

Your golden opportunities will almost always occur in the box, particularly when you can win two or three consecutive games. When this happens, there is a tendency for your adversaries to steam; having only the slightest of advantages, they will tend to double, hoping to pressure you prematurely into surrender. Time after time in instances of this kind, we have seen the box retire on the grounds that he has won enough, that he must not be greedy, that having won two or three games in a row, he should now conserve his new-found wealth. This is not only cowardly but foolish. At such moments the box is being offered what amounts to an emotional double, and instead of dropping he should take. It is criminal to lose your nerve when you are in a hot streak. When the opposing players, falling behind and wrangling among themselves, offer neurotic doubles, the box should accept them with the joy of a man who receives a gift he had not expected. Whenever the enemy is rash, it is a time to attack, not to preserve your gains and retire.

Another point might be mentioned here. The concept of "greed" is sometimes greatly misunderstood. Backgammon essentially is a series of calculated risks. There is no reason to be foolhardy, but don't retrench when you're going well. For instance, assume that you are 100 percent certain to win a game if you play a move a certain way. An alternative way makes you only a 7 to 1 favorite—but you will win a double game if you get away with it. Which play is correct? It's not even close; in a money game, play it the second way every time. You're not being greedy by doing so; you are simply playing the percentages and taking a calculated risk.

After the box has doubled in a chouette, a situation may arise which is called a *drop-take*. In other words, having been doubled, two of the players may decide to accept one double jointly and to drop the other, thereby minimizing their potential loss. Thus, if the box is against two other players and they decide on a drop-take, the box will automatically win 1 point, and with the doubler now at 2, will either win a total of 3 points or lose 1. The two partners will either lose 3 points or win 1. This of course presupposes that there is no further doubling or gammon.

Often there are so many players in a chouette that the box will take a partner in order to lessen his risk. This usually happens when six or more players are in the game; therefore, instead of being one against five, say, it will now be two against four. The box may select any member of the opposing team as his partner, providing the player is agreeable, and this usually leads to the best player in the chouette being chosen constantly. A superior method is to force the box, should he wish a partner, to select the player he has just defeated. There is a pervasive logic in this method; it eliminates any favoritism. When the box can select anyone to partner him, it may be awkward for the chosen player. This is especially true if the nominee is constantly picked. He is not obligated to comply, but it is insulting to refuse. If a fair rotation system is devised, however, none of these unpleasant situations arise.

Depending on whether or not you are a member of the general partnership or on your own in the box, the strategies of your game should fluctuate. As a partner, you should accede to the majority opinion. This should be done even when you feel the wrong percentage play is being made. Given the fickle make-up of the game, the wrong move may miraculously be right; secondly, everyone is playing for pleasure as well as money, and by not voicing your discontent you contribute to the feeling of good will at the table. More importantly, in any game in which you are not in the box, you are playing for only 25 percent of the stake if there are, say, five players. In addition, if all of the captain's advisers object to his proposed move, he should comply with the majority opinion, though if he cared to, he could insist on his own way. These are the manners of backgammon, the game's civilities.

As we have said, you play your most crucial games in chouette when you are in the box. This may seem obvious, but we have seen and continue to witness among the group opposing the box violent arguments, growing occasionally so heated that a player will actually quit and walk away in anger. Since such a player usually stands to lose only a third or a quarter of the total stake, this is absurd behavior; yet wherever chouette is played these altercations occur. Resolve never to indulge in such foolishness; even if a technical error is made now and then, relax and let the captain play it his way. In the long run, you'll save time and avoid petty and unnecessary disputes.

In Europe there is a colorful custom called *giving for games*. Any backgammon player in or out of the chouette can, should he like either side, utter the words "Giving for games." This means that he will give whatever the amount of the doubler is at the moment to any and all participants for their respective games. He does this because he believes a double is in order, and of course he immediately doubles. The participants must either go along with the double or give over their games to the newcomer. It is an ironclad rule. If it is the box that is being doubled, he may preempt any or all the games, giving the necessary points to as many of his opponents as he wishes. Or he may accept the double outright for all the games.

There is a great risk for anyone who makes the offer of "giving for games." He immediately gives the number of points on the doubler to each player and proceeds to play for twice that number. Thus, if he loses (assuming no redouble or double game), he loses 3 units, whereas his maximum profit is only 1. This applies to all the games he has bought, so he must be very sure of the position when offering the proposition.

Anyone already playing in the chouette may also say "giving for games" and take over. The only time the tactic is not permitted is when one side is obviously playing for a gammon.

"Giving for games" is a colorful addition, especially if a few wild early-doublers are loose in the vicinity. Someone will walk in, notice that because there are so many players he will not be able to play for a long time if he starts at the bottom of the rotation, and therefore announces, "Giving for games." If he is fortunate, he will vault immediately into the box. There is more fun than science in this European innovation, and since no one is ever forced to make this highly speculative offer, it has become one of backgammon's more amusing eccentricites.

Contrary to your style of play as a member of the partnership, playing alone in the box should not affect your tactics in any way. You should play against four or five opponents as boldly as against one, and not flinch simply because the stakes are higher. If you are doubled, and it is a double you would normally take, you should take it here. A take is a take; nothing but the position of the game should influence your decision. If the sum involved disturbs you, your abilities are being affected adversely.

The simplest method of determining just what stakes you should play for in chouette is to multiply the stake by the number of players in the game excluding yourself. For example, if the stake is $1 a point and there are four people in the game, you must ask yourself whether you are comfortable playing for $4 a point and whether you will be able to take a double to $8 with equanimity. If you can, play; if not, find another game.

Some years ago in London, a striking example of the stakes you should not play for occurred in a chouette. A man called Gravita was playing against eight other men, most of whom were excellent players. Gravita had been losing steadily for years, but he enjoyed the game and always paid his debts. On this particular evening the stakes were set at £20 (about $50) a point. Toward the end of the evening, Gravita was somewhat ahead, but the game at hand was going against him. The doubler had been turned back and forth to 64, and in mid-game the partnership, sensing an advantage, redoubled Gravita to 128.

Gravita hesitated, then laughed and said, "Well, gentlemen, I can't afford to pay if I drop, so I'll take it." (Had he dropped, his loss would have been $25,576.) Everyone smiled; Gravita was known for his little jokes. But when the game ended, Gravita found that he had lost a double game, or $102,304. He stood up from the table, walked out of the room, and to this day, no one has ever seen Gravita again. As a result, whenever anyone in London takes a bad double, it is known as a "Gravita Take."

◄9►
SETTLEMENTS

It is from the character of our adversary's
position that we can draw conclusions as
to his designs and will, therefore,
act accordingly.
— *Karl von Clausewitz*

Settlements are an important strategy in all money games, and though they are used in European tournaments, they are not as yet allowed in the United States. A settlement is a compromise negotiated between the opposing sides, wherein one army agrees to give up a portion of the disputed stake in return for an immediate end to the hostilities. It is a complicated form of bargaining in which one faction attempts to buy off the other by saying, in effect, "Surrender this much now or ultimately I may take it all." Settlements are the game's politics.

Given the esoteric mathematical hagglings such negotiations involve, many players of backgammon have chosen the simplest course: they never settle. One man of our acquaintance plays regularly in a running chouette. He is a better than average player but knows nothing about this facet of the game and therefore has adopted the tactic of refusing all settlements, regardless of how attractive they may seem. By refusing settlements he reasons that he will at least break even. It is sound strategy, since he is incapable of determining how much he should give or take in specific situations.

But the art of settlements is not as difficult as it may at first appear, and since these proposals to compromise usually occur at crucial moments in the game, a rudimentary understanding of how they work can be beneficial. Settlements may crop up in the middle of the game, but normally they are made toward the end, when the game suddenly takes, or seems about to take, an unexpected turn from certain victory to defeat, or from defeat to possible victory. During these crucial moments, when, for example, the player in the stronger position sees that his superiority may be undermined, or the player in the weaker position can turn the game around by rolling one specific number, players may attempt to reach an immediate compromise rather than risk the whole stake. If a player can determine the precise odds against his winning or losing, in situations of this kind it is not difficult to compute what percentage of the stake he should either take or give.

In all settlements there is a basic formula to use. Take the recurring position in which red is bearing off and leaves a blot which if hit will give white the game. It is a 25 to 11 shot in favor of red. The doubler is at 32. Since white is the underdog, how much should white give? On an average of 36 games, given the odds, red will win 25 and lose 11, for a net gain of 14. If you multiply 14 (his net gain) by 32 (the stake), you get a figure of 448. Dividing this figure by 36 (the number of games played), you get an exact settlement of 12.44. Since 12 is the nearest whole number, 12 is the correct settlement that white should give to red. You will note that the underdog gets a tiny edge here, since he should give 12.44, but this kind of fraction is generally overlooked.

But just because you know the fair settlement is 12 in no way commits you to negotiate that figure. Though it helps if you at least know what the fair figure is, it is not considered unethical to ask for more if you are red, or to offer less if you are white. Both sides are bargaining. Sometimes unfair settlements are intentionally offered; since the less skillful player is either ignorant or confused by settlements, he may accept a lesser amount or surrender a greater amount than the correct figure.

There have even been cases in which the less skillful settler, having been offered *more* than he deserved, has demanded even more than that. In a money game played a few years ago, a position arose in which red had four men remaining on his 1 point and white had two. This position is illustrated in Diagram 75. Red needed any double in order to win the game. The doubler was at 64 on red's side and white offered a settlement. What would the correct offer be?

Thirty shots lose for red and six (the six doubles) win, so he was exactly a 5 to 1 underdog. Again, using the formula—in 36 games, white will win 30 and lose 6 for a net gain of 24. As before, multiply 24 by 64 (the stake), which is 1,536. Divide by 36 (the number of games played) and we get $42\frac{2}{3}$, or, to the nearest whole number, 43. But this was the last game, and for other reasons white was not prepared to court disaster. Thus, in a burst of generosity, he offered to take only 32, 11 points less than he was technically entitled to.

Red was behind and steaming. He considered the proposal, looked up and said, "You want *32?* I'm not giving you anything. As a matter of fact, I'm going to double you to 128." White was amazed, but he shrugged and accepted the double. Red then rolled double 4's to win the game, and red, for the hundredth time, wondered why he had ever become involved in this cruelest game.

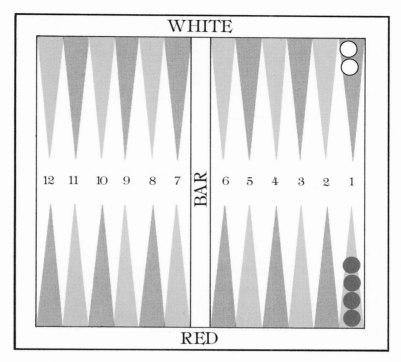

WHITE

12 11 10 9 8 7 | BAR | 6 5 4 3 2 1

RED

Diagram 75

To date, settlements are not permitted in American tournaments, which is unfortunate, for they are a definite part of the game. Should beginners find them difficult, they have only to refuse. In Europe, however, they are allowed and contribute greatly to the game. Recently, in an important London tournament, red, an experienced and wily player, was pitted against a comparative beginner. They were playing a 15-point match with no Crawford Rule, and white was ahead 13–12. The doubler was at 2 on white's side, and the match had progressed to a critical position in a critical game (see Diagram 76). At this juncture, red, whose turn it was, said, "I'll take 1 point." The offer looked and seemed reasonably fair, since white had to roll a double to win. But white was uncertain, and after thinking about it declined the settlement.

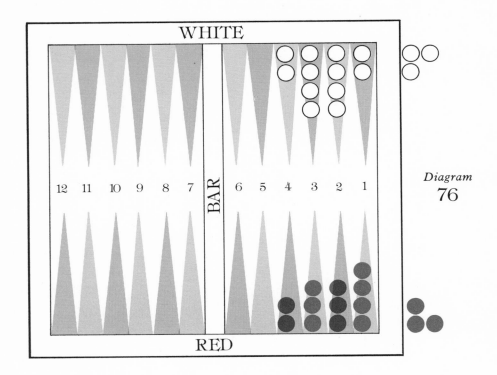

Diagram
76

The game continued and after four rolls by red and three by white, neither red nor white having rolled a double (see Diagram 77), red halted play before white's roll and again made the same offer. "Perhaps I'm foolish," he said, "since it's three rolls later and I'm in much better shape than before. I'm probably getting the worst of it, but I'll still take 1 point." On this occasion white, seeing that red would be off in two rolls and that he still needed a double to win, relented; he agreed to the offer of the point and the score became 13 – 13.

Before reading on, try to determine which of the two got the better of the deal. Was it unfair or fair? It is, in fact, probably the most outlandish swindle imaginable. But why?

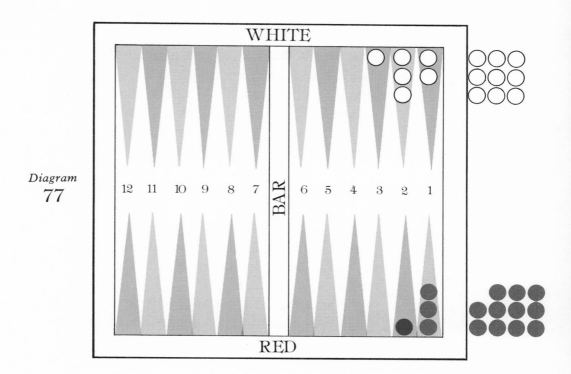

Diagram **77**

Consider the situation. There is no Crawford Rule, so there are no restrictions on the doubler. They are playing to 15 and white is ahead 13–12. If the doubler had been on red's side in any money game in this position, it would be a clear-cut drop. Also in any money game, an offer to take 1 by red should be promptly accepted by white. But in this special instance, white has virtually nothing to gain and everything to lose by conceding a point. What he has failed to comprehend is that this is the game that can win the match. Had white played out the game and lost, the score would have been 14–13 against him. This is no worse than being 13–13, which the score became when the offer was accepted. Behind 14–13, white will certainly double on the first roll of the next game. (You will remember that to be ahead 14–13 is slightly better than being at 13–13, because when your opponent doubles on the first roll of the next game, which he will do, you have the choice of dropping if you wish.) Except for this slight compensation, however, the loss of 1 or 2 points had no bearing on the outcome of the match, and thus for white to concede 1 point and give up the possibility of rolling a double to win the match was lunacy. It is hard to conceive of a more lopsided settlement in favor of red.

Incidentally, there was nothing unethical in red's proposal. It was little more than a political gesture which white was at liberty to accept or refuse. This is what bargaining is all about. The point to remember here is that regardless of how persuasive your opponent is, if you *know* you are receiving the best of it, accept; if not, decline.

To be able to settle well is a form of money management, and the judicious control of one's money is essential in all games of chance. Oddly, correct money management often goes against the odds—and rightly so. For instance, assume that you have $10,000 to your name and no other assets of any kind. You are approached by a man with $20,000 who requires an additional $10,000. He offers to bet his money against yours on the flip of a coin. It is an even-money bet. Would you accept? It is the sort of situation bookmakers and professional gamblers dream about, for you are getting 2 to 1 on an even-money bet. But though the bet adheres to the normally excellent axiom which states that when you have the best of a proposition, bet all you can, it would be folly to accept the challenge. There is another axiom which states that when you are down to your case money, never bet it all on one roll, regardless of the odds you get. Today is important in the world of chance, but not when it eliminates tomorrow.

This is an example of wise money management ignoring the odds. This sound principle is applied particularly in places like Las Vegas, where casinos not only have the best of the odds, but limit the size of your stake as well. It is a sensible practice, since it would be possible for someone on a streak actually to break the house. The limit which the casinos impose on their clientele is an essential form of money management.

In backgammon the same principle should be applied. Be wary of games that become so high and wild that in order to manage your money properly you must take the worst of the odds. Suppose, for example, that you are in a five-handed chouette at $5 a point, a stake somewhat higher than you usually play for, and that the doubler has somehow been turned and turned to 64. You are in the box and are feeling distinctly uncomfortable. While bearing off, you leave a blot. Your opponents have a single shot; it is 25 to 11 against their hitting you, but if they do, they win the game. At this point they offer you a settlement. The correct settlement in this example is 25, but you would take much less; in fact, you would take almost anything you could get. By allowing this kind of situation to develop, you have squandered valuable equity. Avoid these predicaments and play only in games where settling depends exclusively on the position and not on the financial catastrophe that would occur should your opponents obtain the right roll.

In backgammon there are certain "insurance" situations in which players will intentionally take the worst of the odds. This is most frequent in the final matches of a tournament when one player reaches a position whose odds can be calculated exactly.

An example of this occurred in the finals of a recent championship match. Each player had 16 points in a 17-point match, and victory would be decided on the final roll

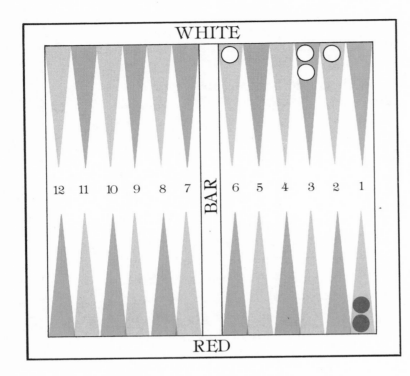

WHITE

BAR

12 11 10 9 8 7   6 5 4 3 2 1

RED

Diagram
78

of the final game. In that final position (see Diagram 78) red, an Englishman, had two men left on his 1 point. White, an excellent player from the Far East, had four men left, one of them on his 6 point. It was white's roll, and so he needed double 6's to win the first prize of $6,500. At this point, red stopped the game in order to take insurance against the possibility of white rolling double 6's—the odds of which, you will recall, are 35 to 1 against.

Red extracted a $100 bill from his pocket, turned to the crowd of spectators and asked what odds he could get. One spectator said he would give red 30 to 1 against the double 6's, and red agreed. Another offered red 31 to 1 against for a further outlay of $100, and again red agreed. Of course red knew he was getting the worst of the odds, but in this case it was worth it as insurance against the potential disaster of double 6's.

It was white's roll, and he promptly threw double 6's to win the match. By losing, red collected not only the $2,500 second prize, but also a total of $6,100 from the two spectators—$2,100 more than he would have received had he won the tournament. As the crowd surged round the table congratulating the players, a woman turned to another spectator and asked, "Aren't the true odds against double 6's 35 to 1?" "No," the man said, "not when a Chinaman's rolling."

◄10►

END·GAME TACTICS

The art of war is largely an art of
manoeuvre. The effectiveness of a fighting
unit depends on the coordination
of its parts.
—*Karl von Clausewitz*

To have the ability to improvise, to deviate when necessary from the norm, is the hallmark of the best backgammon players. Too many others, once they have learned the fundamentals and acquired a certain low panache, play the game for the rest of their lives as though it were parcheesi. This is particularly true toward the end of the game during that last swift sprint into the inner board. We have seen players moving their men as mechanically as a Monopoly counter. Yet the strategies employed at this stage are among the most subtle and important in backgammon.

A case in point is the artful deployment of 1's. In Diagram 79, red rolls double 1's. Red's position is bad, but not hopeless. He is attempting to preserve his board and requires delay. Paradoxically, the way to accomplish this is to rush all four men on his bar into his inner board. This apparently eccentric play prevents red from being forced to move 6's. If any of these four men remained on the bar, it would have to be played down to the 1 point if a 6 were rolled, and red does not want these men out of play. Thus,

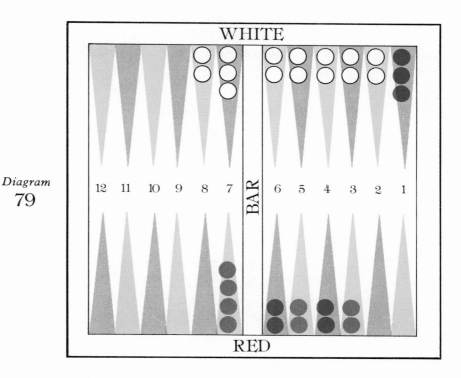

Diagram
79

to cause delay, red rushes his men forward. A contradiction in terms, but correct and logical.

In Diagram 80, very different tactics are required. The situation looks similar but is almost completely opposite. Red is well ahead in a running game, though he has left behind a rear guard of two men on white's bar point. Unless cunning delaying tactics are employed, almost certainly one of these men, and perhaps both of them, will be captured. In this position, red again rolls double 1's. He must now protect himself from being forced to play a 6 from white's bar point. Since he is far ahead in a race, he is in little hurry to put the men in from his bar point. More importantly, he can use them to play 6's and thereby protect the stragglers on white's bar point. The correct play is to move one man from his 6 point down to make his 2 point. In this position red should leave himself as many 6's as he can, the reverse of the tactic of the preceding diagram. In this example most players would tend to make the right move, but would ignore it in the preceding instance. Such plays illustrate the fluid patterns of the game, and variations of these positions occur again and again in late-game tactics. If you learn to apply these concepts in these specific instances, they will strengthen every department of your game.

An extreme example of a paradoxical play occurred in a tournament in Switzerland a few years ago. In a match going to 15 points, the score was even at 13–13. In the penultimate game, red rolled a 5-4 in the position illustrated in Diagram 81. No Crawford Rule was in effect and there had been no double. After considerable deliberation,

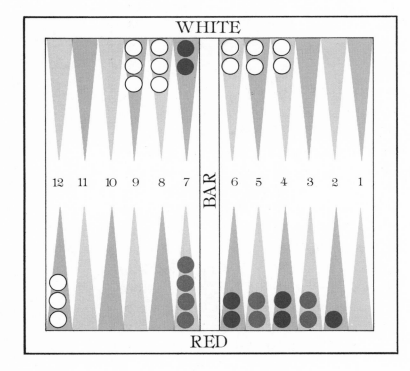

Diagram
80

red moved one man from his 9 point to his 5 point, and
another from his 6 point to make his 1 point. Red could, of
course, have moved his man on white's 5 point all the way
to his own 11 point, thereby escaping white—as white was
quick to point out to red when the game had ended. But
the reasoning in this instance was more involved. To run
and win a single point gave red virtually no advantage except the dubious one of dropping in the next game when
white doubled, as he was bound to do after the opening
roll. By staying and holding his ground, red risked losing
the game, but it also gave him a slight chance of winning a
double game and the match; therefore he thought it worth
the risk. For example, if white had thrown a 3-1 or a 5-3
on the next roll, he would have had to give red a 7 shot,
with perhaps worse still to come. (Of course, white could

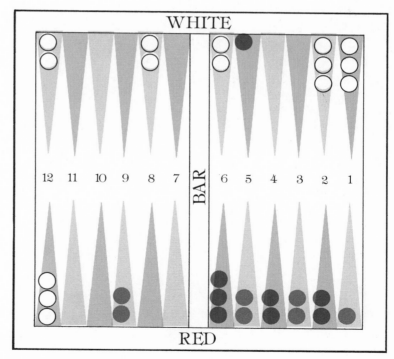

Diagram
81

play two men down from the 6 point with the 5-3, but this would leave him more vulnerable than ever for the rest of the game.) It is imaginative thought of this kind that lifts the level of the game and is yet another example of sound improvisation.

In Diagram 82, red has brought in all his men except one, which remains on white's 9 point, and white has two men on red's 4 point. Red has a 1 to play and has the option of moving it up one point to white's 10 point. Ordinarily the farther a man is from his adversary, the more difficult he is to hit; thus, advancing by one point would appear to give white a slightly improved chance of hitting him. But a little thought will show that leaving the man on the 9 point makes him vulnerable to double 6's, double 4's and double 3's, whereas if he moves to the 10 point, he is

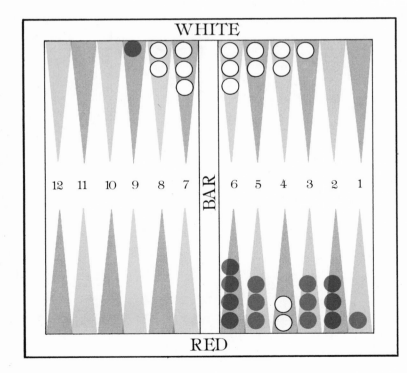

Diagram 82

vulnerable only to a 6-5. So it is correct to move one pip closer.

Examples of this kind may seem minuscule, but if you wish to improve your game, such moves are vital. Nor should such computations deter you. No more than a grade-school knowledge of arithmetic is necessary; given that, you will have acquired a definite edge over the player who tends to scoff at such details.

Another tactic, referred to previously, often escaping the beginner's attention, is hitting *too many* of your opponent's men. Assume that red has a closed board and one of white's men on the bar. If red is still coming around the board and if white has left several blots, red should pick up only enough of them to assure the double game. (Ordinarily four men are sufficient.) Superficially, it would seem safe enough to hit as many of his men as you please. But if you picked up eight men, for example, and then began bearing off, it is quite possible that you would leave a blot. Had white had only four men on the bar, he would probably have come in by the time you had only, say, your lower three points left, but with eight, there is a good chance of his remaining out until you are forced to leave a blot. Hit only as many men as you need, no more. Don't vacuum the whole area; your greed could cost you the game.

In Diagram 83, white has rolled a 5-4. You will remember the rule that if you must leave a blot, you should move your men in such a way as to give your opponent the least number of shots. In this instance, however, the wiser course is to contradict the "percentage play." The play giving red the least number of shots is to move one man from the 6 point to the 1 point and the other from the 5 point to the 1 point, leaving red a 1 to hit; or to move two men from the 6 point, leaving red a direct 2. Each play leaves the least number of shots, but both are unconscionable, since they destroy white's board and in all probability he will be worse off on his next roll. It is better, therefore, to seek an alternate way of playing the 5-4 even though it is less safe. Many players would bring a 5 down from red's 12 point to their 8 point and play the 4 from white's 6 point to white's 2 point, leaving themselves vulnerable to a 1 and to some vague indirect shot (in this case, a 9). But this too would be incorrect. Instead, white should bring both men from the 12 point, one to the 8 point and the other to the 9 point, where he will be exposed to a direct 5 and a 3-2. This play might appear to be less safe, but it is much less dangerous. To give these two extra shots is much safer than giving the 1 and the 9. In the latter, the total number of shots that will hit is 16, whereas in the recommended

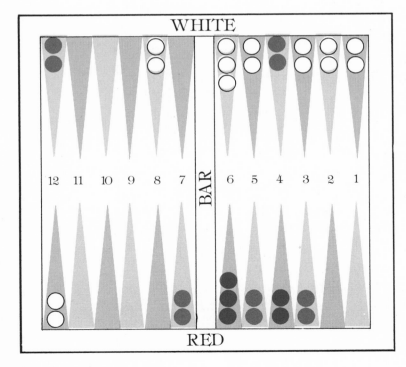

Diagram
83

play the number of shots that will hit is only 13. An additional advantage to this play is that it is easier to transport your blot to safety on the next roll. Again this is an example of a simple mathematical decision which happens in backgammon constantly.

In Diagram 84, white has been forced into what seems to be a frightening decision. White has a 1 to play and red has a closed board. Most players become petrified at the sight of an opponent's closed board and would tend to play the 1 safely behind red's blot. But forget the danger for a moment and examine the logic. If white decides not to hit, red is certainly a favorite to win this game, since he is well ahead in a race. But if white hits, red has suddenly become a 25 to 11 underdog, since he must roll a direct 5 to win

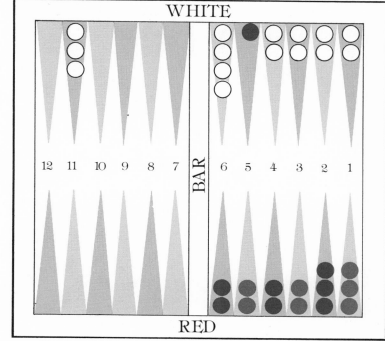

Diagram
84

the game. Thus, white must hit. There is more common sense than courage in this play. The only danger to consider is that white could lose a double game, but it is remote and should not be taken seriously.

Diagram 85 is another example of what passes for bold decisive play. White is on the bar and rolls a 3-1. Many players would enter red's board on the 1 point and use the 3 to save the man on their 9 or 7 point by bringing it in to their inner board. But the move accomplishes nothing and still leaves white dangerously exposed. The correct play is to enter red's board on the 3 point and to hit the blot on white's 5 point by moving one man from white's 6 point to his 5 point, leaving two blots in his board. Once again, there is nothing particularly bold in

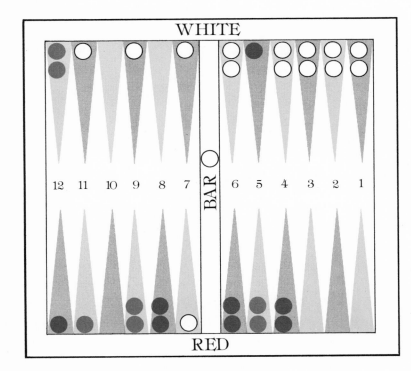

Diagram
85

this play; indeed, not to make it is certain suicide. When white can reduce his chances of being an almost certain loser to being only a 5 to 4 underdog, he is not being bold. But due to the unnaturalness of this tactic, most players would not consider it. However, the play puts red on the bar, and if he does not throw a 5 or a 6 on his next roll, white will have strong double-game possibilities. If red were not hit, he would have complete freedom of movement to assault white's numerous blots and would almost certainly win a double game himself.

But assume that white enters and hits red. Should red now double? In a money game, he should double every time. Under certain tournament conditions, depending to some degree upon the relative abilities of the two players, he should not. Of course there are always special circumstances. If red is the weaker player, he should double even though he is on the bar, because he is trying to use the dice to counteract his opponent's greater ability. But if he is the stronger player, he should not double, since he prefers to have his technique hold sway, rather than the luck factor. To repeat: such decisions are always influenced by the strengths and weaknesses of your adversary.

Often in late-game positions, it is the rolling of small numbers that elicits the most subtle variations of play. In the next three examples, the strategic movement of a 2-1 becomes a crucial factor in the success or failure of red's game. In Diagram 86, white has borne off 13 of his men, and in this position red rolls a 2-1. In this instance there is only one correct play. Whenever your opponent has 13 men off, you must force him to break any point in order to get both of his men on the bar. If he has your 1 point and you have established a prime, break the prime so that he has to play a 6 if he rolls it. Red should move one man from his bar point onto his 5 point and the other from

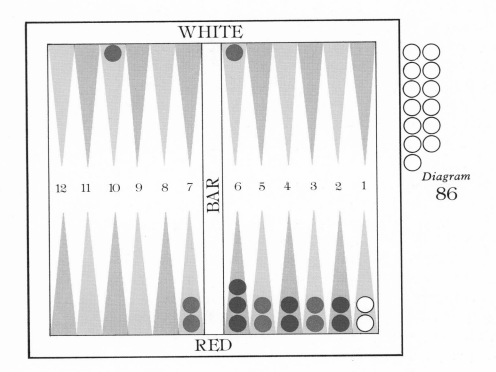

WHITE

12 11 10 9 8 7 BAR 6 5 4 3 2 1

Diagram
86

RED

white's 10 point to the 11 point. Of course, double 6's may win the game for white, but they would win the game anyway if red waited to break his bar point until all his other men were in his inner board. Further, by leaving one man on his bar point, red increases his chances of winning, since he will come in again in white's board if white throws a 6. The chief principle at work here is that all risks are worthwhile in order to separate white's two men.

Again, in Diagram 87, white has borne off 13 men and established a point in red's board. Red now rolls a 2-1. The principle is the same as in the previous diagram; red must force white to break his anchor. The correct play is to move one man from white's 4 point up ·to his 6 point and to move the 1 from red's 5 point to red's 4 point, leav-

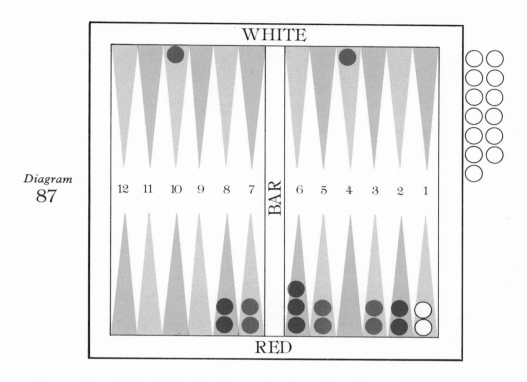

Diagram 87

ing two blots in his inner board. This play gives white 3's and 4's to move, and red hopes that white will be able to hit one of his men. The oddity of this play should not deter the beginner. It is logical and the strongest threat to white's position. It also shows that red has devoted some thought to his game and is alert to the potentialities of all rolls.

In Diagram 88, white has borne off 12 of his men and has established a forward point in red's board. Red now rolls a 2-1. In this instance red appears to have several options, but again there is only one logical move. Red could hit the blot on white's 4 point, but should not do so, since his object is to break white's anchor. Almost any number will cause white to do so, whereas if red hits, white will

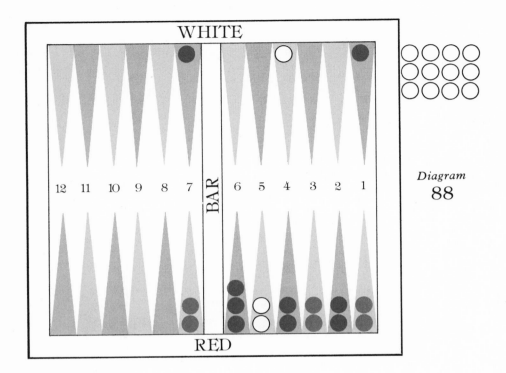

Diagram
88

have to wait for 5's in order to re-enter — which will be to his advantage. Here the logical play is not to hit, forcing white to run. Once that happens, red is in an excellent position to capture all of white's three remaining men. When this is accomplished, he may double and white should drop. Red's best play is to move the man on white's bar to his 10 point.

In conclusion, there are many late-game positions involving the tactical deployment of two separate men — especially when you have borne the rest of your men off the board. In positions of this kind, beginners seem particularly confused and tend to push their remaining men toward the 1 point with gloom and resignation. For example, in Diagram 89, red has two men left in his inner board

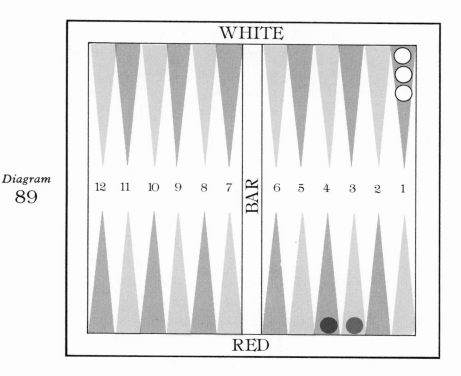

Diagram 89

on different points, having borne off the rest of them. White has three men left on his 1 point. Red has a 1 to play. In this situation a dilemma almost always arises as to where to move the 1 in order to have the best chance of taking both men off on the subsequent roll.

A general rule: with two men left, it is never wise to double up — that is, to place both men on the same point. It is usually better to move the front man forward. In the position shown, red is a 19 to 17 underdog to take both men off on the next roll. The 1 is crucial here. To move from the 4 point to the 3 point is irrelevant, since the same number of shots will get both men off next time. Red might just as well have left the man on the 4 point. (This applies to any two men doubled up on the odd points — for instance, the 5 point. You might just as well have one man on the 5 point and the other on the 6 point; the same number of shots will bear both men off on the next roll.) The play, therefore, is to move the man on the 3 point to the 2 point, making red a 23 to 13 favorite to take both men off on the subsequent roll.

With two men remaining in your inner board, always tend to go toward the 1 point with the front man. The only exception to this is if you have one man on the 6 point and the other on either the 2 or 3 points. In both these cases you should always move the man off the 6 point.

The paradoxical nature of backgammon is seen most clearly here. Take 7's, for example. In the following three diagrams, red has in each instance two men left, and it is

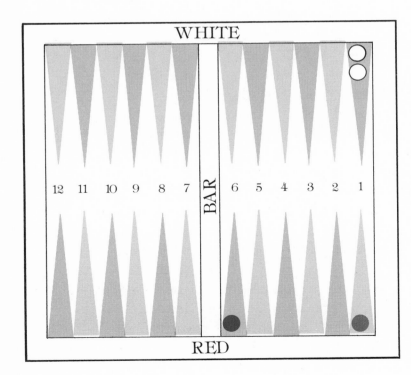

Diagram
90

his roll. In Diagram 90, he has one man on his 6 point and the other on his 1 point; in Diagram 91, he has one on his 5 point and the other on his 2 point; in Diagram 92, he has one on his 4 point and the other on his 3 point.

In Diagram 90, red is a 21 to 15 underdog to take both men off in one roll. But if the back man is one pip farther forward, and the front man one pip less advanced, as in Diagram 91, red becomes a 19 to 17 favorite to bear both men off. Yet if they are still closer together, as in Diagram 92, red becomes a 19 to 17 underdog. If one were to employ the pip count in each case, a total roll of 7 would get both of red's men off, and yet the odds of bearing them both off vary considerably. This is just one more indication of the pip count's inherent fallacies.

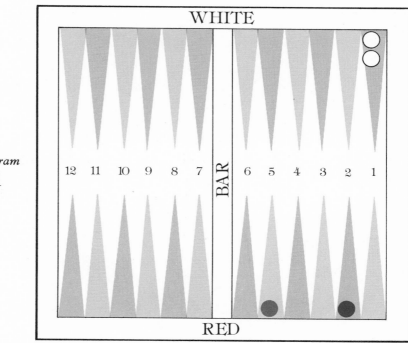

Diagram
91

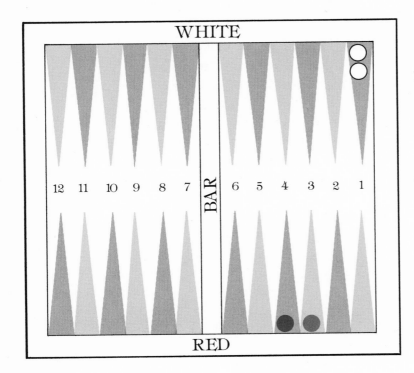

Diagram
92

As has been demonstrated, all late-game play involves astute tactical ability and a talent for making the right percentage play. In these final stages of the game, when one combatant often has his back to the wall, there is no room for guesswork, and if you follow percentages and adhere to the inherent logic of the game, you will rarely have to guess. Let your opponent guess. To guess in an either-or position is to make a mistake exactly 50 percent of the time.

◄11►
THE PSYCHOLOGY OF THE GAME

All war supposes human weakness and
against that it is directed.

—*Karl von Clausewitz*

There are many reasons for
the tremendous resurgence of backgammon, but one aspect of the game in particular makes it unique. There is no other game involving skill in which the beginner after a short time reaches a level from which he has a definite chance to beat anyone else, no matter how good his opponent. This is a built-in hazard for the experienced player, a great boon for the newcomer and adds excitement for kibitzers and participants alike.

The rules of the game are simple, their execution an art; this is backgammon's pervasive principle. However, it is the game's apparent simplicity that is its greatest attraction. Almost anyone can learn 60 percent of the moves in a week, and we know of no one who did not believe that he actually understood the game in a few days. But backgammon is so subtle that it may be impossible to learn *all* there is to know about it. One of the world's leading players, who has played for thirty years, admits that he probably understands only 90 percent of the game. As you must know by now, backgammon is more complex than it first appears to be.

Because of the subtle skills involved (most average players believe those who are better than themselves are lucky), and because most players tend to rationalize the dice, blaming their misfortunes on "bad luck," it is difficult not only to recognize your mistakes, but to evaluate your abilities. The game is usually played for money, and self-deception can be expensive. Given the luck, the self-deception, and the fact that there is no other game in which a player can so often make the wrong move and win as a direct result of it, backgammon has become for many of its devotees an exquisite siren song, a honeyed land of hope and double 6's. It is for these reasons that we have called backgammon the cruelest game.

Like some concealed and irreplaceable mechanism, cruelty *is* built into the game. For example, it is replete with paradox. Once the dice have been thrown, a battle begins, and each succeeding roll will alter the position, the tactics and the strategies. Certain basic theories, all sound, may have to be violated at any time. It is this elusive principle that is probably the most difficult to comprehend—and the most destructive when it is not brought into play. The beginner will learn the fundamental rules—and will then be told that he must contradict them. Though many players acquire other more mechanical skills, they never completely grasp this. But it is this flair for improvisation which separates the average player from the expert. A good player is one who plays his bad rolls well. A chronic loser loses because he is unable to play his difficult rolls to his best advantage. Anyone knows how to bear off four men when he has rolled double 6's.

All too often the wrong computation, the wrong decision, and hence the incorrect move will win. This is the most unkindest cut of all. But it happens so often that players who have won as a direct result of it attribute their success to skill and believe the game requires no further study. Backgammon is glutted with such people. If one attempts to explain certain percentages to them, they are merely insulted. When they lose in money games or tournaments, they will later confide to intimates that their opponent was unbelievably lucky and their own dice unbelievably bad.

In this aspect, no other game can be compared to backgammon. For example, if you challenged Bobby Fischer at chess, and for some reason he accepted, you would not win a single game. In bridge, an inferior player will seldom win a tournament, and in poker the best player will almost always win.

Except for chess, there is an element of luck in the above games. In backgammon, however, the luck factor is dominant. Though many of the percentages in backgammon are calculable, the ratio between luck and skill remains obscure and has probably been discussed for as long as the game has existed. Because it is not as logical as chess or as scientifically exact as checkers (a game so restrictively formal that if two experts play, the one who moves first always wins), it is often dismissed by the unknowing as just one more game of chance performed by gamblers who might just as well be flipping coins.

Although the ratio of skill to luck is impossible to compute exactly, it is generally agreed that when the adversaries are evenly matched (both technically and emotionally), the game is all dice. Over the short term, an average or good player can beat a superior player, but in the long run even the "unlucky" expert will win, for the law of averages is as infallible as the law of gravity. We believe that the proportion of luck to skill in backgammon is approximately 80 to 20, but a 20 percent edge is an insur-mountable advantage.

Take Las Vegas. If you play craps against the house and play correctly (that is, giving yourself the best chance), the percentage in favor of the house is actually less than 1 percent. But given that minuscule advantage, in the long run the house will win. In comparison, the 20 percent skill factor in backgammon is overwhelming.

As another example, what possibilities exist for horse-players when the track takes 15 to 17 percent out of every dollar they bet? None. You can only win consistently at the track if you have somehow fixed the race or have managed to obtain inside information. In backgammon, an understanding of the correct percentage moves in specific situations qualifies as "inside information" and will enable you to win in the long run. But not every time, alas, and often not even in what you believe to be crucial games. This condition must be accepted philosophically, of course, and should not deter you from continuing a detailed study of the game.

Backgammon is not a game in which luck should be taken seriously, though many players continue to gamble at it, apparently relying on the spurious advice of the Oriental sage who claimed that if you threw a lucky man into the sea, he would emerge with a fish in his mouth. Such players forget that though *they* are gambling, the experts are not. Gamesmen rather than gamblers, the experts always have an edge because they know infinitely more about the game. Like many other endeavors, backgammon is a game of levels; to play against the experts for money is nothing more than another version of Russian roulette.

Backgammon might be compared to *Alice in Wonderland*. On one level, that book can be described as a droll fairy tale, but among the childish games, improbable characters and laughter there is a subtle allegory that tells an altogether separate tale. In much the same way, backgammon can be learned and played forever as a rather simple game of chance: once it is taken seriously, however, cunning labyrinths and curious paradoxes begin to appear. This book has attemped both to teach the beginner how to play and to enjoy the game, and to present at least a few of the game's more intricate conundrums.

A note about kibitzing: If you are not directly involved and are watching a match, no matter what happens at the table—repeat, no matter what—say nothing. Form any opinion you wish about the play or players, but remain silent. Should some flagrant error astonish you, steal quietly away. When the match is over, but not until then, you can approach either contestant and raise your questions or objections, but never during play.

If an argument arises between the two players and you feel sure you know who is in the right and can show why, still say nothing—unless, and this is vital, you are appealed to by *both* opponents.

Over the years, at tournaments and in money games, we have seen specific positions presented to experts who will then argue the relative merits of the "right" move. Rarely do they agree. At the end of these discussions, each man will go his separate way convinced, however secretly, that he was right and the rest of them were wrong. Backgammon seems not only to attract but to elicit the most outrageously egotistical behavior. If, for instance, a confidential questionnaire were sent to thirty acknowledged experts and each was asked to fill in his choice for the one best player in the world, you would get thirty different nominations, all autobiographical. More often than not, the expert was not sure that he was right, but being an "expert," he was expected to take a stand, which he will uphold for illogical reasons.

In bridge, for example, upon analysis the correct percentage play can almost always be determined, but though there are positions in backgammon where the proper move is self-evident, there are countless others where it is almost impossible to get a majority opinion. In Diagram 93, for example, red has rolled a 6-4. What is the correct move? There are at least three good options, but expert opinion is invariably divided.★

Which is as it should be. The game has few absolutes. It is fluid and ever-changing, and often the best that one can hope for is to sensibly exercise specific options. It is a game of calculated choices, which may be as humdrum or

★First, you could cover your 2 point with the 4 and play the 6 in to your 5 point. White cannot escape on his next roll unless he rolls a 6-5, and even then he is vulnerable to a return 6-1. The reason for this choice is not that it is conservative but that it *forces* white to move. Any double is awkward, and should white not roll a 5 or a 6 he will (except for 2-1) have to put builders out of play or weaken his five-point prime.

Secondly, you could hit white's blot on your 3 point, using a man from white's 12 point. This play leaves two blots in your board. It is true that white also has two blots, but these do not concern him much because he has a five-point prime, and every man of yours that is hit will have to get first to his 4 point and only then follow with a 6 to be free. If you choose to hit in an effort to keep the lone white piece from escaping, you could be defeating your own purpose because he may be prevented from moving at all, which could be to his advantage.

The third choice would be to hit his blot with the 4 from your bar point and to come out to his 10 point with the 6. This is wild, wide-open and imaginative, but it makes the next roll crucial. White could annihilate you, or could be destroyed himself, depending on the dice. There is style and boldness in this play, and if circumstances and the score are such that winning a gammon happens to be more advantageous to you than losing one is disastrous, you should consider taking this plunge.

Which of the three should you pick? An unequivocal answer is impossible. But this very fact is why backgammon is such a fascinating game. Of course it is frustrating not to know for certain what to do. You *know* that you should make your 5 point with an opening 3-1, but as you progress you must learn to improvise to the best of your ability, and the longer you play, the more aware you will become that a countless number of inscrutable dilemmas like this example will occur.

Size up your opponent, the situation (is this a tournament or for money? head-to-head or chouette?), and the score. Try to weigh every angle and then choose what is best, considering the circumstances. We are not hedging when we say that a sound argument could be made for each of the three moves above, depending on the situation.

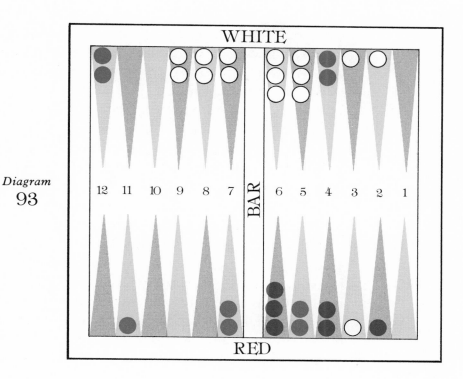

Diagram
93

eccentric as one wishes, but need not necessarily be "correct."

There is also a certain amount of gamesmanship to be employed in backgammon. As in any other competition, it is never advisable to appear nervous or uncomfortable when you sit down to play. This is particularly true when you are opposed by a well-known player. Never greet him by saying, "You're too good for me. I'm only a beginner and don't have a chance against someone like you." There is only one instance when you can say this: when you don't mean a word of it! Given the uncertainties of the game, you always have a chance, and with determination and the dice you can upset the most expert of players.

If you tend to play slowly—and at first you probably

will—don't be intimidated by an opponent who rushes his moves. Take your time, no matter how much he hurries you. Attempt to play your routine moves with a certain steady rhythm and without hesitating needlessly—but only when you feel secure in doing so. As you improve, you will grasp the problem created by each specific move more quickly, and so make your plays with assurance and finality. Occasionally, of course, there will be a difficult decision with which you'll have to take some time, and this is to be expected; in general, however, try to develop the habit of making your mind up fast and react accordingly.

The board is comparatively small, and your position and your opponent's are in front of you at all times, so try to avoid "balks." When part of your roll is "forced"—that is, if you have a 5-4 to play and there is only one 5—move this 5 immediately, and then concentrate on the best deployment of the 4. Many players will roll the dice and immediately play the number, but having done so, they will retract the move and make another play elsewhere, then vacillate again and make yet another move. Soon they are back to where they began and in a quandary. Sometimes it's difficult to choose the best percentage move, but try to train yourself to avoid this kind of play by thinking the situation through before touching your men. What it boils down to is simply mental discipline, which is as valuable in life as it is in a game. This sort of intangible is a valuable asset every time you sit down to play.

Size up your opponent immediately. Attempt to estimate his strengths and weaknesses. If he is more experienced than you, use every legal ploy you have to equalize his edge. For instance, you should attempt to make every game as simple as possible. Against better players, always seek simple positions. Block and run as best you can, and at all times avoid back games. Further, if your opponent attempts to needle you, remain impervious. If he stalls, allow him to do so without becoming irritated. If he talks, try not to listen, nor to fall into conversation. Concentrate on the game at hand and ignore anything that intervenes. Check all of your opponent's moves and remember that it is not considered unethical to allow him to place his man in the wrong spot if it is to your advantage. In short, display as little emotion as possible, and try to disregard bad luck or the fortune which may seem to favor the enemy. The good player is one who does not compound his losses with personal feelings. "And yet," as one expert has said, "99 percent of the people who play double up when they are losing and draw back when they are ahead. You must look at backgammon in the same way that you would look at a business reversal over which you had no control." Of course this is a question of discipline—but discipline is a quality that can be learned.

There is an interesting and complex psychological factor at work in the taking or dropping of a double. Assume that in a chouette over a period of a few months certain players dropped 1,000 games in which they were doubled, and were correct 700 times and wrong 300, none of which was a gammon.

For many people the actual money gambled is not the primary incentive. They enjoy the challenge and want to win more for winning's sake than for receiving financial rewards. Such people like to be proved correct; it is part of their pleasure and boosts their egos. If you were able to look into these players' minds and psyches, you might find that they actually *preferred* to be correct in their decisions 70 percent of the time, even though they are subconsciously aware that if they had been *wrong* 70 percent of the time (that is, if they had accepted all the doubles), they would be better off financially. The droppers of those thousand games are minus 1,000 units; if they had taken, they would be minus 1,400 + 600, for a net of minus 800.

Many takable doubles are dropped because of such an outlook. Perhaps in these cases the individual is receiving emotional fulfillment amply compensating him for his lower financial rewards. We are not arguing for or against such eccentric behavior; we merely state that it exists and occurs in many more instances than is realized.

As mentioned earlier, the ego is rampant throughout the backgammon world (probably more unjustifiably than in any other game, since the dice are the controlling factor), and the desire to be "right" is neither consciously recognized nor admitted by most players. It is a factor worth thinking about, though, and perhaps there is a latent streak of it in all those people who drop too soon. The point is, those players who drop takable doubles are paying out good money that they don't have to lose.

When you do lose—and you will—try hard not to say that your opponent out-lucked you. Nobody particularly cares that you missed two triple shots and that your opponent hit a 17–1 shot to win the whole match. But if the provocation *is* too much and you must moan a little, *never* tell your opponent that he played a move incorrectly. Even if it is true, what have you gained? Restrain yourself, congratulate him and contrive to smile! This is important, because regardless of how good you are, you're going to gain considerable experience in being a loser.

Conversely, when you win, attempt to be gracious; if you have been lucky, admit it. No matter how badly your opponent behaves, neither argue nor disagree; after all, you can afford to be generous.

The discipline that pervades the game should also control the amount of money for which you play. This may seem too obvious to dwell on, but more than a few players involve themselves in high-stake games which invariably meet with the predictable conclusion. If the amount of money you are playing for makes you uncomfortable, you should not be playing for that stake. That is the key to what you should play for. What you can "afford" is not necessarily the stake at which you feel comfortable, whether it is high or low. The two can be quite different. Assume that you are a millionaire many times over. You can "afford" to play for almost any stake, but the chances are that you would be uncomfortable long before you reached the sum you could not afford. The amount to play for is that which does not divert your attention from your main concern—the game.

This is not a lecture on how to conduct a life style or an attempt to dictate the stakes you should play for. Our sole purpose is to help you play in the most comfortable frame of mind. Whether or not you have a fortune, if the stake distresses you, simply decline to play in that particular game. If you allow your ego to get the upper hand and are seduced into a bigger game, you are at a distinct disadvantage. You may out-luck it and win, but in the long run you are a favorite to lose because you will inevitably drop doubles that you should take, or not double when you should, for fear of increasing the stakes. Why expose yourself through false pride to such a situation?

To sum up: the stake that permits you to play at your best is the stake that permits you to relax—regardless of what you can afford.

What we have been primarily concerned with in this chapter are the psychological traps into which every player has periodically fallen. It is to these specific traps that we wish to direct your attention, since if they are not recognized and remedied, your backgammon talents will not progress beyond mere technical expertise. An eminent neuropsychiatrist and analyst believes that to win at any game, you must first understand the specific skills involved, and secondly the specific traps—that is, the psychology of the snares laid by your adversary. If you have mastered neither the skills nor the trap's alternatives and still insist on entering the game, you are throwing a razor-sharp boomerang which will ultimately cut off your own head. The psychiatrist goes on to say that the professionals of any game are those who place their opponents in various categories, and then apply the trap most likely to seduce them. It is the failure to recognize these traps and the subsequent inability to exert some rational control over the course of events that not only indicate but instigate disaster.

This is yet another of the game's paradoxes, and perhaps its most important one. It is a game of war, a series of all-or-nothing skirmishes conducted for the most part in civilized company toward civilized ends. It is what Nick the Greek, that most infamous of American gamblers, had in mind when, in discussing expert game-playing, he said, "It is the art of polite bushwhacking." Given the scope of backgammon and its infinite possibilities, it is the consummate encounter.

◄ 12 ►
THREE GREAT GAMES

The common denominator of war
is the duel.
— *Karl von Clausewitz*

The following game took place between two of the best players in the country, and illustrates much of what has been stressed throughout the book—for example, the vital importance of both 5 points. To obtain these, inordinate risks should sometimes be taken, and when both of them were secured, these two fine players held them tenaciously, no matter how tempting the inducements that were offered in an effort to break them.

Note also these players' ability to improvise, and to adjust their thinking to the constant flux in their respective positions. Risks are taken here, safe plays made there, and always the percentages are weighed.

In addition, the tremendous value of "owning" the cube is graphically displayed in this game. This all-important part of backgammon cannot be overemphasized. It has been stressed again and again in the chapter on doubling, and here, in the end game below, is a practical demonstration of what we have been trying to point out.

This specific game, played for high stakes, drew an audience, and though the two opponents happened to be friends, the ego factor began to emerge, as it usually does when a crowd gathers, so both players gave it their best. The result is backgammon of the highest caliber, full of imagination and expertise on both sides, and the reader cannot help but learn from it if he plays it out, move for move, on his own board.

1. **Red** opens with a **6-1** and makes his bar.

1. **White** rolls a **4-1,** moving one man from red's 12 point to his own 9 point, and starting his own 5 point.

2. **R—5-1:** moves the 5 from white's 12 point to his own 8 point and drops the 1 from his 6 point to his 5 point. Both players are correctly trying to make their respective 5 points.

2. **W—6-6:** makes his own bar with two men from red's 12 point and establishes his own 2 point with two men from his 8 point. This roll is too much too soon, but what else can he do? It would be wrong to break the 12 point here.

3. **R—5-4:** hits white on his 5 point with man from his 1 point and keeps going out to white's 10 point. He would prefer to make his own 5 point, but since he can't, he is at least preventing his opponent from making his.

3. **W—4-2:** enters on the 2 point and hits red's man on the 5 point with man from red's 1 point.

4. **R—5-4:** here red could enter on either the 4 or the 5 point and continue on to hit white on the 9 point, but instead chooses the correct tactic of entering on the 5 and then making this point with the man from the 1 point.

4. **W—4-2:** white in turn makes his opponent's 5 point with man from red's 1 point and starts his own 4 point with man from his 6 point. He is leaving two blots in his outer board because he is trying to lure red off his own 5 point. Once again, an example of correct expert tactics which are seldom, if ever, followed in average competition. (See Diagram 94.)

5. **R—2-1:** starts his own 4 point with man from his 6 point and moves man from white's 10 point to white's 11 point, leaving 2's everywhere. At this moment red doesn't mind being hit, and this play gives him diversification.

5. **W—4-3:** moves the blot from his 8 point and covers his own 4 point, and starts his 3 point by moving off his 6 point. He is still leaving the blot on his 9 point to try to tempt red to break the vital 5 point.

6. **R—4-3:** red correctly refuses the bait. With man from 8 point he covers the blot on his 4 point, and plays the blot on white's 11 point to his own 11 point. With this he is vulnerable to a 6, but to his opponent's cost of breaking the 5 point. (Alternatively, this roll could have been played from white's 11 and 12 points to red's 10 point, thus

Diagram
94

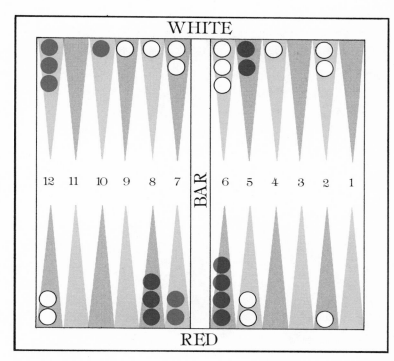

blocking white's 5's. This move also has merit, and some experts might prefer it.)

6. **W — 5-3:** with the 3 he moves from red's 2 point to the 5 point, and finally saves the man on his 9 point by moving it in to the 4 point. To come out all the way with the back man would leave red with too many options.

7. **R — 5-3:** moves the blot on his 11 point all the way to start his 3 point.

7. **W — 5-4:** moves one man from red's 5 point all the way to his own 11 point, making him vulnerable to a 6. But at what cost to red!

8. **R — 5-2:** moves both men in from his 8 point, covering his 3 point and improving his board. Since white is clinging tenaciously to his 5 point, red's 8 point has little value at this stage.

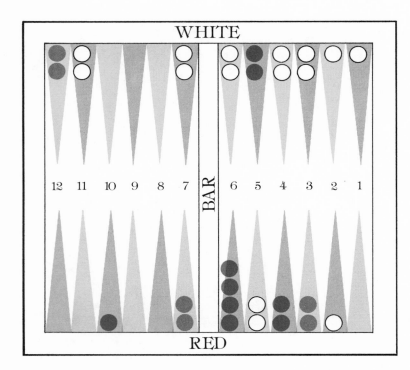

Diagram
95

8. **W — 2-1:** There are some interesting choices here. White's is to cover the 3 point in his board with the 1 and to play the 2 from red's 12 point to his own 11 point to block red's 6's. By doing so he gives three extra shots (4-4, 5-3, 3-5) at the blot on red's 12 point, but considers that blocking red's 6's is worth it. He could also have moved all the way from the 11 point to the 8 point, leaving only a 3, but in our opinion his move was much superior.

9. **R — 2-1:** hits white's blot on the 12 point with man from white's 12 point and continues on to his own 10 point. A questionable play. It might have been better if red had split off his own 6 point; there's no need to take any risks at this particular stage of the game. This is perhaps the only error by either player in the game, and it is a minor one. Still, unless white gets the "miracle roll" of double 5's, it is doubtful that he would break his anchor to hit red were his next roll, say, 5-1 or 5-2.

9. **W — 2-1:** enters on the 2 and plays the 1 from his own 2 point to his 1 point. Playing the 1 in this way is virtually forced, but these two open blots in white's home board will strongly affect the strategy of both players henceforth. Indeed, red promptly doubles because of these two open men in white's board, and because white's timing is bad. White accepts. (See Diagram 95.)

10. **R — 4-2:** brings the blot in from his own 10 point all the way. He doesn't hit white on his 2 point because if white does not roll a 6 or a 3, he may have to play a man or men elsewhere in the board he does not want to move.

10. **W — 4-4:** moves two men out to red's 9 point, at last breaking the 5 point, and two men from his 11 point to his bar. An awkward shot, but at least he has men to play now.

11. **R — 4-3:** hits white's blot on his 2 point with man from his 6 point, and moves out to white's 8 point with the 3, leaving 2's everywhere. A roll of 2-2 by white now

would be a disaster, but the risk is worthwhile. To move the 3 from his own 6 point to his 3 point would of course be safer, but it is awkward and craven.

11. **W—5-3:** enters on the 5 point and continues out to the 8 point. A good shot for white; if he had been forced to hit red's blot on the 2 point and not been able to cover those in his board, it could have been the beginning of the end.

12. **R—4-1:** hits white's blot on the 8 point with a man from white's 12 point. Red is going all out offensively now because of white's two blots, and is correct in his decision not to make his own 2 point.

12. **W—6-5:** enters on the 5 point, and with the 6 is at last able to cover one of the blots in his board. (See Diagram 96.)

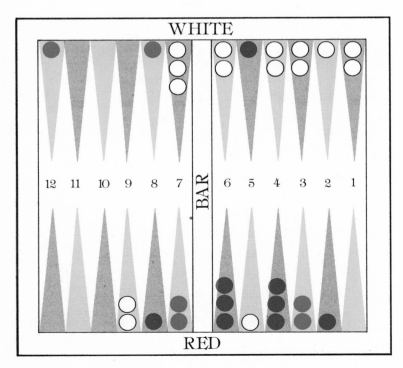

Diagram 96

13. **R—5-3:** There are several choices here. For instance, red could cover his 2 point from his bar point and hit white's blot on the 5 point, but this would leave five blots open around the board, and if he were hit and could not come in, even for a single roll, he might lose a gammon. Instead he rightly chooses to play conservatively, covering his 8 point with the 5 and making white's 8 point with the 3.

13. **W—5-4:** moves out to red's 9 point with the 4, and covers his own 2 point with the 5, establishing a five-point board.

14. **R—4-1:** covers his 2 point with man from his bar, establishing a four-point board.

14. **W—3-2:** brings one man in all the way from the bar, leaving one man out so that he won't be forced to play a possibly awkward 6 from red's 9 point.

15. **R—6-5:** makes his own 1 point with men from his 6 and 7 points. He could run with one of his back men, but this is risky—particularly because there is no assurance that he will be able to get by next time, and may have to leave an 8 again.

15. **W—5-4:** moves all the way from red's 9 point to his own bar point.

16. **R—5-2:** moves one of the men on his 8 point all the way in to the 1 point. He too is leaving a man out, just as white did earlier, in case he has an awkward 6 to play.

16. **W—5-2:** this time white plays both men in off his bar, figuring that red on his next move will have to either break his board or move off white's 8 point. White wants to keep his board intact in case he gets this indirect shot.

17. **R—4-4:** moves the two men from white's 8 point to the 12 point, and two men off the 6 point to the 2 point, still leaving himself a playable 6. (See Diagram 97.)

17. **W—6-3:** a very interesting decision for white:

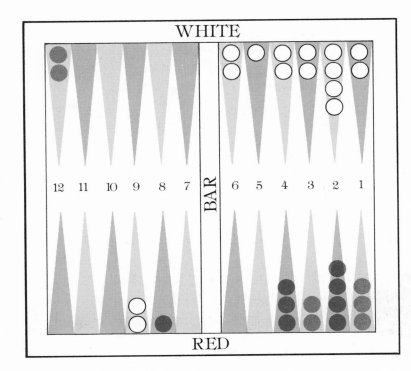

WHITE

| 12 | 11 | 10 | 9 | 8 | 7 | BAR | 6 | 5 | 4 | 3 | 2 | 1 |

RED

Diagram
97

should he leave a 1 shot or a 4 shot? If he leaves a 4 and is not hit, red is slowed up drastically unless he gets both men on white's 12 point past white with a very good roll. Yet to leave a 4 shot instead of a 1 is giving red 4 extra chances (15 instead of 11). After much reflection, white decides that red's position in a potential race is too strong, so he leaves the 4 shot and plays one man all the way to his bar.

18. **R—5-2:** white's play pays off. Red has to play a man from his 8 point down to his 1 point.

18. **W—3-2:** moves his back man safely to his own 11 point.

19. **R—5-1:** moves both men off white's 12 point to red's 12 and 8 points.

19. **W — 5-1:** moves both outside men onto the 6 point.

20. **R — 5-2:** moves the man on the 12 point all the way in to the 5 point.

20. **W — 4-1:** takes a man off his 4 point and his 1 point.

21. **R — 4-2:** moves his last man in from the 8 point to the 4 point and takes a 2 off.

21. **W — 4-3:** takes two men off.

22. **R — 6-1:** takes two men off.

22. **W — 3-2:** takes two men off.

23. **R — 6-2:** takes two men off.

23. **W — 6-2:** takes two off.

24. **R — 4-1:** takes two off.

24. **W — 5-2:** takes two off.

25. **R — 6-5:** takes two off.

25. **W — 2-1:** takes two off.

Up till now, both players have rolled fairly well in bearing off, considering that there have been no doubles, but though red has been slightly in the lead all the way, his advantage hasn't been really clear-cut until now. But white owns the doubler and red can do nothing but roll and hope. The advantage of having the cube on your side is graphically illustrated here. If it was red's turn to double and he did so now, white would be hard put to accept, but since white has the doubler, he is in this game till the very end and cannot be forced out.

Look at Diagram 98 and note that there is yet one more fascinating paradox here. With three men on the 6 point, 3-3 would be a better roll for white than 4-4, even though the latter roll has 4 more total pips! This is one more example of the distortions of the pip count.

26. **R — 5-4:** takes two men off.

26. **W — 5-1:** takes one man off his 6 point.

27. **R — 3-1:** takes two men off.

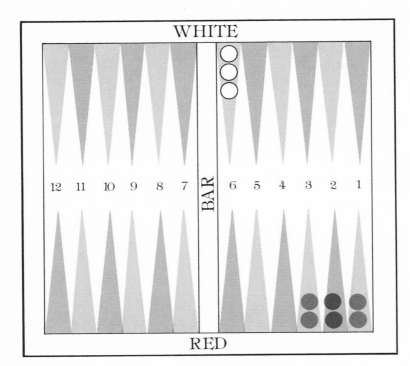

WHITE

12 11 10 9 8 7 BAR 6 5 4 3 2 1

Diagram
98

RED

27. **W — 4-4:** wins the game on his last shot with his only double. Only 6-6, 5-5, 4-4 or 3-3 win for white in this position, making him an 8 to 1 underdog, but as is so often the case, because he had the cube he was able to hang in to the end and pull the game out at the last possible instant.

◄►

A few years ago during a pause in a major tournament in the Caribbean, two of the top entrants challenged each other to a few head-to-head money games. After all, what else could they do for relaxation? One of their games was the following, and it is worth close study.

1. **R — 5-2:** moves two men over from white's 12 point.

1. **W — 3-3:** makes his own 5 point and moves two men up to his opponent's 4 point to thwart red's builder on the 11 point.

2. **R — 3-3:** also makes his 5 point and moves up in his opponent's board to the 4 point. An alternative would be to block white's 6's by moving two men to red's 10 point, but his play is better.

2. **W — 4-3:** hits red's blot on the 11 point with man from red's 4 point. A good play, because red can now only hit white with 4's and 2's anywhere in the board.

3. **R — 4-3:** enters on the 3 point and hits white's blot on his own 4 point with man from his 8 point. He should not even consider for an instant breaking his anchor on white's 4 point and hitting white's blot on the 8 point.

3. **W — 2-1:** enters on the 1 point and saves his blot on the 8 point by moving it in to his 6 point. White must retrench at this moment because he has no defense.

4. **R — 3-3:** There are lots of choices here. Red chooses to make the 3 point in his own board with two men from his 6 point, to hit white's blot with his own blot on the 1 point, and to bring a man down from white's 12 point to his own 10 point. This is a great shot, for if white fails to enter, it will be extremely hard for him to accept a double in light of his open man on red's 11 point.

4. **W — 4-3:** enters on the 4 point and hits red's blot on white's 3 point with man from his 6 point. It is mandatory for white to hit here in order to try to keep red busy, thereby protecting his open man on red's 4 point.

5. **R — 6-2:** enters on white's 2 point and hits white's blot on his own 4 point with the 6. Note that had white not hit red in his previous roll, the 6-2 would have pointed on white here.

5. **W — 6-3:** cannot enter.

At this point red gives a good gambling double. He has gammon possibilities, and white's position is perilous. But white daringly takes in this position; he is perhaps showing off a bit because of the audience. (See Diagram 99.)

6. **R—6-5:** red covers his 1 point with man from his 6 point and starts his bar with man from white's 12 point. He is going all out to blitz white if he doesn't enter on his next roll.

6. **W—6-4:** a saving shot for white. He enters on the 4 point, hitting red's blot, and continues on out to the 10 point.

7. **R—6-2:** enters on white's 2 point and starts his own

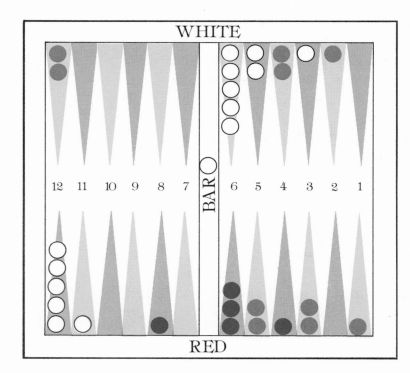

Diagram
99

2 point with man from his 8 point. He does not save the open man on white's 12 point because suddenly he needs badly to delay; having made his own 1 point, he is far too advanced at this stage of the game.

7. **W—3-2:** covers the 3 point in his own board with man from his 6 point and hits red on the 12 point with the 2. This is a close decision, but red's board is now just good enough so that white feels he should avoid giving a direct shot.

8. **R—5-2:** enters on the 2 point and continues on out to the bar. Again, he does not make his own 2 point because he is ahead of himself.

8. **W—5-5:** hits red on the bar with man from his 12 point and makes his 8 point with three men from red's 12 point. He does not make his 1 point because he wants red to come in and be forced to play.

9. **R—6-2:** has to enter on the 2, and to avoid breaking his forward anchor must play the 6 from his 7 point to his 1 point. Red is now in a very bad position. (See Diagram 100.)

White now correctly redoubles. It is a bad emotional take by red—but he takes nonetheless, as happens with even the best of players from time to time.

9. **W—4-4:** a great roll. Makes his bar with the man on red's 10 point, and makes the 9 point with the two men on red's 12 point, establishing a five-point prime.

10. **R—4-1:** moves two men off his 6 point, making the 2 point. This could have been worse; he still has a four-point board.

10. **W—6-4:** moves both men in off the 9 point.

11. **R—5-2:** a tremendous saving shot for red, giving him a chance. Needless to say, he moves the back man off the 2 point all the way out.

11. **W—6-4:** brings both men in off the bar.

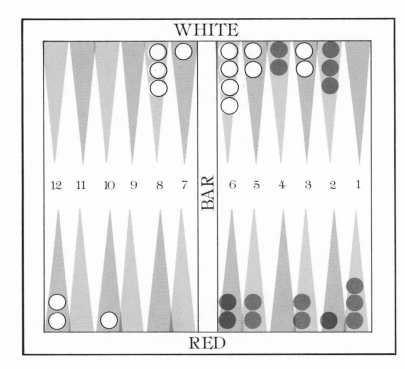

WHITE

BAR

12 11 10 9 8 7   6 5 4 3 2 1

RED

Diagram
100

12. **R—3-2:** moves from white's 9 point to his own 11 point.

12. **W—5-4:** moves his forced 4 from his 5 point in to his 1 point, and the 5 from his 6 point also to the 1 point. By moving the 5 this way rather than bringing it in from outside, white still has two builders to bear if red decides to break his forward anchor.

13. **R—6-1:** starts his 4 point by moving all the way from his 11 point.

13. **W—5-1:** moves the 5 from the 8 point in to the 3 point, and the 1 from the 6 point to the 5 point.

14. **R—4-3:** moves a man from the 4 point out to white's 11 point. Red feels that he can't afford to spoil his board any further and must break his forward anchor.

14. **W—6-2:** has no 6, so moves the 2 to the 1 point.

15. **R—4-1:** makes the 4 point with the 1, securing a five-point board, and moves the 4 from white's 11 point to his own 10 point. (See Diagram 101.)

15. **W—5-1:** There are a wealth of fascinating critical decisions to be made with this roll. White could hit on the 4 point and move a man in from the 8 point. But this would leave two men open, which is dangerous, considering red's five-point board. Secondly, he could play both outside men, saving one and leaving only one man open to a 3 or a 5. But white chooses to play conservatively and safely, taking both men off his 6 point.

16. **R—4-2:** a good shot. Red starts both 6 points.

16. **W—6-6:** cannot play.

17. **R—2-1:** again a tough choice. Red finally decides

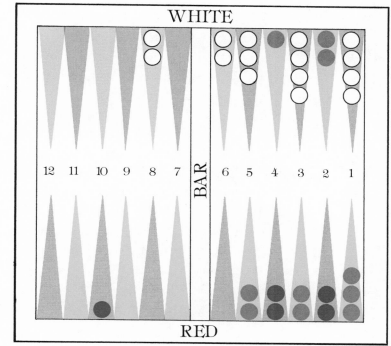

Diagram
101

to come out all the way to white's 9 point, relying on his back anchor to get a shot later.

17. **W—2-1:** another intriguing decision. The best immediate percentage for white is to give red a 2 shot by starting the 4 point, but on his next roll he might not be able to cover, and might even have to leave two men open. In these circumstances white decides to move one outside man to his 5 point and gamble against a 6 — a 20 to 16 shot in his favor because 3-3 doesn't hit.

18. **R—1-1:** moves from white's 9 point to red's 12 point.

18. **W—4-2:** moves the outside man in to the 4 point with the 4, and moves a man from his 5 point to his 3 point, leaving four men on his 5 point. If he left five men there, a 6-6 or 5-5 on the next roll would leave two blots.

19. **R—6-4:** covers the 6 point, giving him a closed board, and moves the 4 to white's 6 point.

19. **W—6-3:** takes a man off the 5 point and saves the blot by moving it to the 1 point.

20. **R—5-3:** moves from W6 to R11.

20. **W—5-1:** takes two men off.

21. **R—1-1:** moves from R11 to R7.

21. **W—3-1:** takes two men off.

22. **R—5-1:** moves from the bar to the 1 point, pinning all his hopes on getting a shot on the next roll, for with his next 6 he will be forced to leave.

22. **W—4-1:** has options, but must leave a blot. Taking another man off is desirable, but not at the cost of giving red two extra shots (2-1, 1-2) if he leaves the blot on his 5 point; therefore he moves both men down, the 4 to the 1 point and the 1 to the 4 point.

23. **R—3-2:** hits the blot on the 4 point and moves on out to white's bar.

23. **W:** cannot play.

Red now redoubles in this position. He is a favorite

here because white has only five men off. But because of
the men on red's 1 point, white accepts the double, for the
chances are that red is going to have to break his board
immediately without getting any of the extra men off *before* he has to break. White's take is correct in all money
games. (See Diagram 102.)

24. **R—3-1:** from W7 to W11.

24. **W:** cannot play.

25. **R—2-1:** from W11 to R11.

25. **W:** cannot play.

26. **R—6-4:** moves his outside man all the way to the
1 point, justifying white's take even more.

26. **W:** cannot play.

27. **R—4-1:** bears one man off the 4 point and moves
the other man down to the 3 point. Red doesn't leave a blot

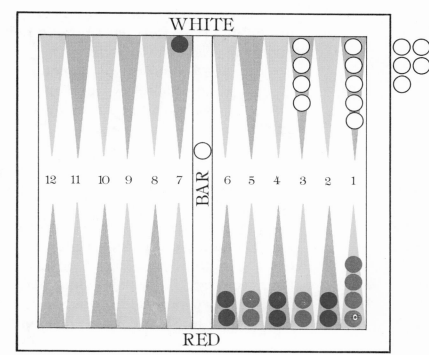

Diagram
102

because he has a chance to win even if white rolls the 4 immediately—though of course 4-4 would probably be disastrous.

27. **W—2-2:** cannot enter.

28. **R—2-2:** takes two men off his 2 point, and moves two men down from his 6 to his 4 point.

28. **W—4-1:** cannot enter.

29. **R—5-4:** bears one man off his 5 point and saves the other by moving it to his 1 point.

29. **W—5-5:** enters on the 5 point and goes all the way to his own 5 point. This "miracle" roll puts white right back in the game.

30. **R—6-1:** takes two men off.

Should white redouble now? Though he has only five men off to red's six, it is his roll, and if he can continue to take two men off on each subsequent roll, he will win the game, barring doubles. But under no circumstances should he redouble at this stage. Any 2 ruins him; besides, with a minimum of five rolls remaining (if neither player throws a double), it is much too early.

30. **W—6-5:** takes two men off.

31. **R—6-4:** takes two men off.

Once again white waits and doesn't redouble, for then any 2 would lose him the game.

31. **W—5-1:** takes two men off.

32. **R—6-3:** takes two men off. (See Diagram 103.)

Now white redoubles, at exactly the right time; he has not waited too long. On the other hand, red must take; any 2 except double 2's will win outright for him because white certainly could not accept a redouble should he now roll any of the ten losing shots (2-1, 2-3, 2-4, 2-5, 2-6, or their reciprocals). By redoubling here, white is admittedly forfeiting two probable further rolls for a chance to win with a double, should he now be unfortunate enough to

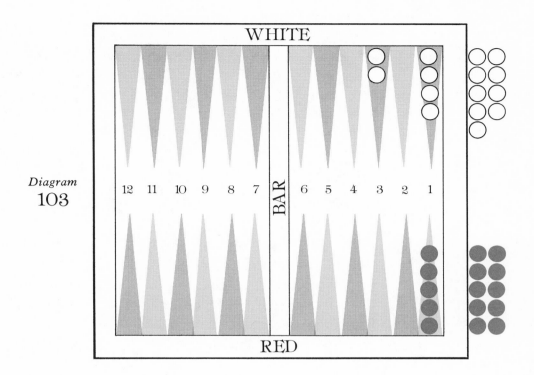

Diagram
103

roll a single 2. (That is, if white did *not* double here and then proceeded to roll a 2, red could not redouble him, since he would not own the cube, and white would have two turns to win by rolling a double.) In fact, certain expert backgammon mathematicians disagree with a redouble here. Perhaps they are right, but since there are players who would actually drop, albeit incorrectly, in such a position, on balance we believe the redouble to be sound. In this instance, Red accepts.

32. **W—3-1:** takes two men off. Now (assuming no doubles) only a 2-1 will lose for white.

33. **R—6-5:** takes two men off.

33. **W—5-4:** takes two men off.

Red now needs any double to win, and is a 5 to 1 underdog. The doubler is at 16, and the stake is $5 a point. How much should red offer, and how much should white accept, to settle their game here? You have all the equipment to work this out, so why not see if you can come up with the answer before reading further? (If necessary, refer to the chapter on settlements.)

In this particular situation, red offers to give $50, and white counters by stating that he will take $60. These offers show that both men know what they are doing, because $50 is too low and $60 is too high. They haggle for a while, and finally settle on $55, which is about right. The nearest figure is between $53 and $54, so white receives a little bit the best of the settlement.

Even though both opponents in this game were fine players, it shows how the emotions can sometimes take over and affect anyone's reason. In particular we feel that red was wrong in accepting white's redouble on the ninth move—despite the fact that in this book we advocate the philosophy of taking a double whenever there is a doubt. But red's position at this stage was almost untenable, and he should have dropped, as most good players would have. Hence, in this particular game justice was done, because after this foolhardy take, red did not deserve to win.

◄►

What follows is a game recently played by two of the world's best in a tournament match in London that was televised and followed with great interest by players around the world.

White opened the game with a roll of 6-1 and made his bar point. Red rolled a 6-4, running out from white's 1 point to white's 11 point. White rolled a 5-2, hitting red's two blots on his 11 point and 1 point. Red then rolled a 5-1, coming in twice and hitting white's blot on the 1 point. A hitting contest then ensued, with each player attempting to establish a position, being hit, and forced in turn to hit again. The moves are listed below.

3. **W — 5-6:** enters on red's 5-point and hits red's blot on own 5 point with man from 11 point.

3. **R — 2-1:** enters on white's 2 point and hits white's blot on own 5 point with man from 6 point.

4. **W — 3-4:** enters on red's 3 point and hits red's blot on his 5 point with man from 1 point.

4. **R — 5-6:** enters, hitting white's blot on his 5 point, and continues on to white's 11 point.

5. **W — 3-2:** enters on red's 3 point and hits on white's 11 point with man from red's 12 point.

5. **R — 2-1:** enters on white's 2 point and hits on own 5 point with man from 6 point.

6. **W — 4-2:** enters on red's 2 point and hits on red's 5 point with man from his 1 point.

6. **R — 3-1:** enters on white's 3 point and hits on own 5 point with man from 6 point.

This was the first really major decision in the game. (See Diagram 104.) Red's option was to come in on the 1 point, establishing two blocks, and to hit with the 3 from his 8 point. But the move as played is imaginative and daring. If red had come in on the 1 point, he would have been committing himself to a back game. Red can afford the play he made because white has made only his bar and has not yet made any points in his inner board. Hence, red is not necessarily in a back game as yet. The drawback to this play, however, is that red has lost a builder by hitting white's blot from his 6 point instead of from the 8 point. Nonetheless, this is an interesting example of early tactics.

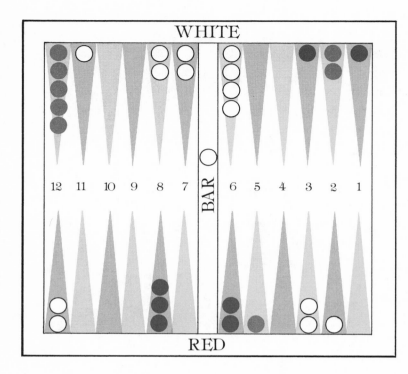

WHITE

12 11 10 9 8 7 BAR 6 5 4 3 2 1

RED

Diagram
104

Red has decided against a back game this early in the game — going along with the theory that back games should if possible be avoided.

7. **W — 3-1:** enters on red's 1 point and hits blot on red's 5 point with man from 2 point.

7. **R — 1-6:** enters on white's 1 point and starts his own bar point with man from white's 12 point.

8. **W — 6-1:** makes own 5 point with men from 6 point and 11 point.

By far his best choice. He, of course, could have hit red's blot on the bar point, but this would serve no purpose, since white has too many of red's men in his inner board already.

8. **R — 3-1:** moves from white's 1 point to white's 4

point and makes his own bar point with man from his 8 point.

Another interesting play. (See Diagram 105.) Red might have left the blot on his bar point and made white's 4 point instead. Another alternative would have been to hit white's blot on red's 5 point with the 3 and to make the 3 point in white's board with the 1. But both of these moves would commit him to a back game, which he is still reluctant to get involved in. But because white now has his 5 point and a four-point block, we believe that red should have made the move. However, we imagine that red, seeing that white had four men in his inner board, was still attempting to avoid a back game. In this case, we feel he was wrong. White's four back men do give him good tim-

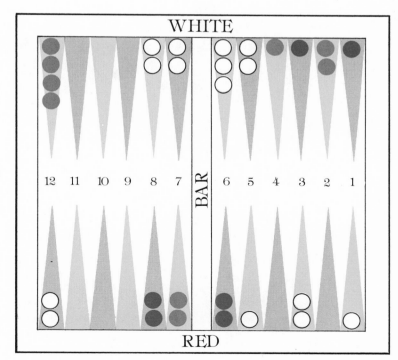

Diagram
105

ing to defend a back game, however, and red decided against it.

At this point, white doubles red to 2. It is interesting to speculate on whether or not white would have doubled if red had used the 1 to make white's 4 point. Despite the fact that white has a good position, it is still a bold double. Red has no serious flaws in his game. He has a defensive anchor and opportunities for delay, and white is short on builders in his outer board. Red must have felt the same, since he accepted white's double.

9. **W—5-3:** makes own 3 point with men from his 6 point and 8 point, hitting red.

9. **R—6-5:** cannot enter.

10. **W—3-3:** makes his own 4 point with two men from his bar point and moves one from red's 12 point to white's 10 point and one from red's 1 point to red's 4 point. (See Diagram 106.)

There are many ways of playing these double 3's. With two of red's men on the bar already and a four-point board, white could have made the 1 point, thereby sabotaging red's back game entirely. Admittedly it is an awkward and unnatural move to make, but well worth considering in this instance. But having rejected it, white surely should have started his bar with the fourth 3, rather than the weak and aimless move up to the 4 point in red's board.

10. **R—3-1:** enters on the 1 point. A great roll for red; he still has one man on the bar, but he has secured that vital second point in his opponent's board.

11. **W—2-2:** moves two men from red's 3 point to red's 5 point, one from red's 12 point to white's 11 point and one from white's 10 point to white's 8 point.

11. **R—4-1:** enters on 1 point and moves from white's 12 point to his own 9 point.

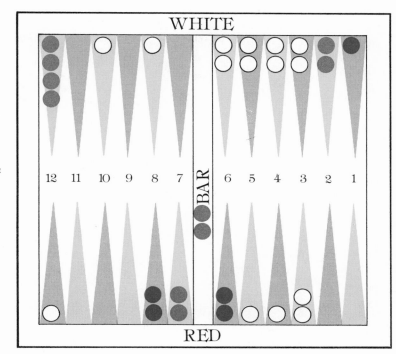

Diagram
106

12. **W — 5-2:** moves from red's 5 point to red's 12 point, not hitting red's blot with the man from red's 4 point. This is the correct play. White does not want to delay red further and so declines to hit. At this juncture, he has a distinct edge in every area. He even holds his enemy's 5 point.

12. **R — 3-1:** red hits white's blot on red's 12 point with man from white's 12 point and moves the 3 from white's 12 point to his own 10 point. (See Diagram 107.)

This is one of the most fascinating decisions of the game. If white's two men on the 5 point had been on the 4 point, we are sure that red would have blocked his 9 point with the 3-1, thereby containing white's three men in his inner board unless white rolled a 6. In this position white

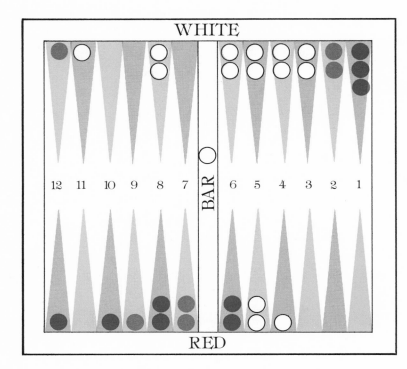

Diagram
107

has very little in reserve and might easily be forced into breaking his blockade. But since the men were on the 5 point, red elected to go into a massive back game. An ingenious and daring play.

13. **W—4-3**: enters on 3 point and moves from red's 5 point to red's 9 point, hitting red's blot. White still does not relish hitting, but in order to break up red's countering blockade, he decides to attack. If he had entered on the 4 point and played the 3 to his own 8 point, he could be blocked with low numbers. Double 3's would be especially disastrous. A good example of going against the usually sound premise of not hitting in a back game. The situation is unique, and white correctly improvised.

13. **R—5-5**: unable to enter.

14. **W — 2-1:** moves men on red's 3 and 4 points up to his 5 point. White might have hit two more of red's men, but rightly decided to bring two men up. An expert play.

14. **R — 6-1:** enters on 1 point and springs to white's bar point.

15. **W — 5-2:** moves from red's 5 point to red's 10 point, hitting, and from red's 9 point to red's 11 point. Here again, white makes a crucial error, in our opinion. The 2 is vital. Following the practice of not hitting when you are defending against a back game, white does not hit twice — but he should have. It is a time to ensure that red does not make white's bar point by rolling a 6-1, 6-2 or 5-2, a total of six shots. (He should not use 5-1 to hit, because the 2 point is too valuable.) It is a calculated risk, but we think white was in error here. If white secures his bar and establishes a prime, he has an excellent chance to contain his opponent's men long enough so that red's remaining forces will be well out of play. In other words, red's other men will have been forced to move to the forward points in his inner board before white's blockade breaks.

15. **R — 5-2:** enters on the 2 point and makes white's bar point. Because white did not hit twice and red did roll the 5-2, he has come from far behind and is about even money now. (See Diagram 108.)

16. **W — 5-5:** moves two men from red's 5 point to red's 10 point, one from red's 11 point to white's 9 point, and one from white's 11 point to white's 6 point. A very cautious play. What is white afraid of? He wants to be hit, and by playing safely he has made himself too fast.

16. **R — 5-3:** moves his two men from his 8 point to his 5 point and 3 point, deliberately leaving two blots. It is entirely to his advantage to be hit, and if white rolls 3's and/or 2's, he will have to hit or strip his board. Curiously, since white does not want to hit under any circumstances,

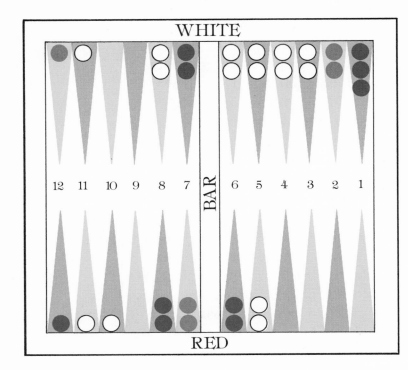

WHITE

12 11 10 9 8 7 BAR 6 5 4 3 2 1

Diagram
108

RED

red is partially "blocking" white with his two separated blots.

17. **W—6-2**: moves from red's 10 point to white's 9 point, and from white's 6 point to white's 4 point. Again white is dogging it by playing safe. Red has perfect timing now.

17. **R—6-3**: moves from white's 1 point to white's 10 point, leaving yet another blot.

18. **W—6-4**: moves from red's 10 point to white's 9 point, and from red's 10 point to white's 11 point.

18. **R—4-1**: moves from red's 12 point to red's 8 point, and from red's 7 point to red's 6 point. There is no point in hitting; he has no board.

19. **W—5-1**: moves from white's 9 point to white's 8

point, and from white's 11 point to white's 6 point, refusing to hit, of course.

19. **R—2-2:** red's first usable double of the game; he uses it to make two good points in his board (i.e., one man R7 to R5, one man R8 to R4, and one man R6 to R4).

20. **W—6-1:** moves from white's 9 point to white's 8 point, and from white's 9 point to white's 3 point. A good shot, but red's timing is still excellent.

20. **R—3-3:** covers the man on his 3 point (W10 to R3), giving him a four-point board.

21. **W—6-4:** moves from W8 to W4. He cannot play a 6.

21. **R—5-4:** W7 to W11 and W12 to R8.

22. **W—3-1:** W8 to W5 and W4 to W3, not hitting. He

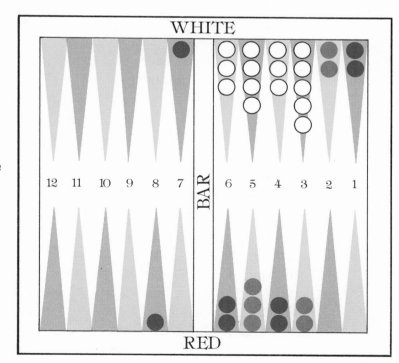

Diagram
109

does not want to delay red.

22. **R—5-4:** W11 to R5.

23. **W—5-3:** W8 to W5 and W8 to W3.

As can be seen in Diagram 109, white has now brought all of his men into his inner board, but red's timing remains nearly perfect.

23. **R—3-1:** R8 to R7 and W7 to W10.

24. **W—5-2:** bears one off the 5 point and moves from W6 to W4.

24. **R—4-1:** W10 to R10.

25. **W—1-1:** W6 to W5 twice and W5 to W3.

25. **R—6-2:** R10 to R2.

26. **W—5-1:** bears one off the 5 point and W4 to W3, keeping his men as diversified as possible.

26. **R—5-1:** R7 to R2 and R5 to R4.

27. **W—4-2:** bears one off the 4 point and W5 to W3 — a forced move.

27. **R—4-1:** W2 to W7.

28. **W—5-4:** bears two men off and leaves a triple shot which endangers two blots. (See Diagram 110.)

In this position, red redoubled. Should white take? In all money games, the answer is yes. Red can hit with any 2, 3 or 4, which means that 27 shots hit and 9 do not, making him exactly a 3 to 1 favorite. You will recall that 3 to 1 is the dividing line on whether or not one accepts a double. In this instance, white is neither over nor under. But the determining factor here is that if red misses, white has good double-game possibilities, since he has five men off already. But because this was a tournament match, and due perhaps to the score at the time or the psychological blow he had just been dealt, white thought it expedient to drop.

When a position like this arises — that is, when you leave a triple shot — do not throw up your hands in the be-

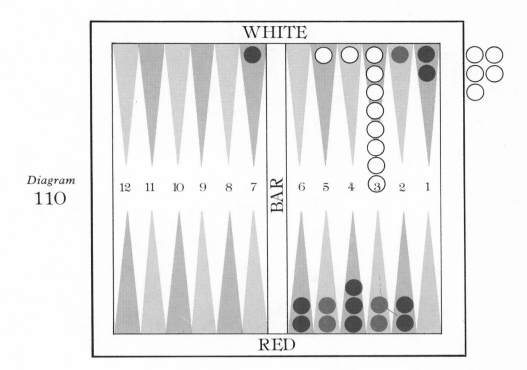

Diagram
110

lief that your cause is hopeless. How many times, for example, have you failed to enter a three-point board? In this instance the odds are exactly the same. But red may have bluffed white here. The psychological setback of suddenly leaving two blots may have caused him to drop without considering the position carefully.

Nevertheless, overall this is a superb game by two great strategists, and it demonstrates the essence of backgammon.

About the Authors

BARCLAY COOKE was born in 1912, and graduated from Yale in 1934. For a year thereafter he worked as a roustabout in the oil fields in the South, then for a bank in New York City, but when he found that this job interfered with his attendance at Yankee Stadium, the Polo Grounds and Ebbets Field, he left with no regrets.

Though Mr. Cooke is widely acknowledged to be one of the three or four best backgammon players extant, he feels that his true métier is as a big-league baseball manager, a post which will never be offered him.

Mr. Cooke is married, has four children, and lives in Englewood, New Jersey, and during the season can be found in the second row of the Metropolitan Opera orchestra every Friday night.

JON BRADSHAW was born in the United States in 1937 and has lived in England for most of his adult life. He is an amateur backgammon player, a professional writer, and the author of *Fast Company*, a comical study of the good works and bad habits of six American gamblers.